Contents

Introduction

WHO WE ARE and perhaps even more important is who we think that we are differs greatly from the perception of other individuals that we encounter on a daily basis.

At certain times during my early life, I thought that I was all that and sliced bread as the saying goes. It took me from my birth in 1950 until the year 2005 to realize that my thinking throughout my life was all wrong. For some lack of life experience or my own mindset, I thought that everyone in the world thought and processed information in the same way as I did. This thought process was a grave mistake on my part. In 2005 while on assignment for the federal government, I had the pleasure of working with a team that opened my eyes to the fact that that there are many different ways of looking at the same problem, or issue, and all of them were valid. So who's to say that my point of view in my book is correct? Certainly not me because I've learned that my point of view is not the only point of view, nor is it the correct point of view.

My book isn't about making you rich but by applying my basic principles you may become rich. My book is about applying basic principles to take you from one level in society to perhaps the next level.

My strongest belief is to always leave a place better than what you found it. In some cases, it boils down to a simple task of picking up litter left by others and placing it into the trash can. Doing for others with no expectations of being rewarded for your deeds but just the sheer satisfaction of knowing that you have improved a common area should be just reward in itself.

By the same token, it is lights and flowers that will deter crime in certain communities. Most of us overlook the simple fact that if you take care of the small stuff, the big stuff will take care of itself.

The old saying is that for every great man, there is a woman behind him pushing him forward. My current significant other is the world of support and constructive advice in all that I do. One of her favorite sayings is that "I aspire to greatness." If anyone can project a person to go forward on their dreams, it can almost certainly be attributed to the positive reinforcement of others that impact our lives.

In closing my introduction, I would simply like to say that I want to believe that anyone buying or reading my book also aspires toward greatness. Because they've recognized something about my book that, perhaps, could alter their lives in some positive way.

We individuals have the power to determine our own path going forward into the future. All is based upon the paths that we choose. The acceptance or rejection of the great advice we receive from others. The applying or demising of our own successes and failures will, overtime, determine the greatness or failure that we will or not achieve during our lifetime.

We, as all human beings do in this world, have the ability to change the dynamics of our current life and circumstances. We have the ability to change or alter any preconceived notions of who we are and what we can achieve during our lifetime.

Some of you have made some bad dissensions in the past, and with that, you have gained a reputation that is holding you back. You can't change the past, but you can change the future. If you were to move out of state and start anew, you would not have a past. Your new life starts with you creating a new past in the new area. The new community only knows the past that you are creating in their community. No one needs to know about your old past. If you decide to share your old past with your new friends, then you might as well just shoot yourself in the foot because you're only defeating your own progress.

Basically, what you should be looking to do is level the playing field for your success. Someone once said, "It's not what we have achieved, or not achieved in our lives. It's all about the journey that we were on."

Most of us have heard the saying that "you only get one chance to make a first impression." That first impression can leave an indelible mark on someone else's perception of who you are and what you're all about. Ninety percent of another person's perception of whom, or what we are all about is based upon the visual presentation that we present to them. Why would you want to shoot yourself in the foot?

Basically, what I'll be addressing in this book was taught to all of us back in elementary school. However, it seems that millions of us have forgotten that education. What I'm alluding to is general hygiene, the way we dress, and the way we verbally express ourselves. If I were to meet you out in public with my hair disheveled, wearing a wrinkled shirt, and torn jeans looking like I just rolled out of bed, then your opinion of me is going to be less favorable. You might even go as far as to dismiss anything that I have to say based upon that thirty-second visual opinion you formed about me.

I think that you'll agree with me when I state that perhaps the single largest group of offenders of the dress code are teenage boys between the ages of fourteen to nineteen. This also just happens to be the period prior to them becoming men, going off to college, or getting the first full-time job. This book has been designed to bring to the attention and educate boys and young men that are even in their '30s and '40s that were never taught the proper way to dress.

There isn't a doubt in my mind that the fifty-percent divorce rate, which started to take place in the late '70s and continued to grow well into the 1990s to peak and hold for a few years. With the father figure gone from the home, the information bridge was broken. That father-to-son communications and teaching was lost. Today, most of these children are now in their '30s to late '40s and were robbed of learning proper manners, how to dress for what occasion, and correct hygiene practices.

Because history has a tendency to repeat itself, I wasn't shocked to find that at the end of WWII (1934–1945; American Involvement 1941–1945), we had experienced a very high divorce rate in America. Most of you young men reading my book might not remember the Vietnam Conflict (1945–1976; American Involvement 1965–1975). Just as the end of WWII saw an increased divorce rate, so did a raise of divorce repeat itself at the end of the Vietnam War. Contributing to the absence of father figures has nothing to do with the divorce rate but that our young fathers were sent off to fight both wars. Both factors figure into a lack of father-son information not being passed down. Not all our young men were affected by the lack of not having their fathers around because they emulated their grandfathers, uncles, older brothers, or positive stepfathers that filled that void.

Allow me to flip the script and present a different image for you of a young man dressed in a highly starched white shirt, ironed khaki slacks, wearing, highly polished reddish loafers, a matching belt, and leather-band wristwatch. Of course, his hair is combed, and he's wearing cologne. I think the visual speaks for itself. Not only would you look favorable upon this person, but you might even entertain the idea of drawing this person into an engaging conversation.

Quality never goes out of style, and if you spend a few extra dollars up front in the long run, you'll actually be saving money. I could go out and buy a dress shirt for $15, and after the first few washes, it will look like garbage, buttons will start falling off, and the seams could even rip open. But if I purchased a dress shirt for $30, it could be 100 percent cotton, have single-needle stitching on all the stress points, and will come with buttons sown into the front tail that I'll never have to use, and after fifty washings will still look brand new.

The goal of my book is to have it serve as a survival guide for young men: to acquaint them with the laws of attraction and the doors that will swing open for them by following my advice. I hope to explain the tools and practices of proper hygiene, how to identify quality clothing at bargain prices through tips, techniques, education, and knowledge deliver a new way of life message. "It doesn't cost a million to look a million" is designed to be informative, educational, witty, antidotal, and is filled with helpful practical quotes.

Chapter 1

Why, or Why Not?

WHO KNEW THAT heroin sheik or grunge was a mainstream fashion style or look. I certainly didn't, yet it was that very look that prompted me to write this book. If style is defined by that measure, then we have really lowered the bar, and perhaps anything goes today, like wearing work clothes to apply for an office job. I guess we can just about mix anything with anything and the presentation just doesn't matter anymore.

Let's face it. The world just isn't fair. Certain people seem to get a pass in life. They seem to get the best jobs, the best service, and all the lucky breaks. Perhaps, you're saying to yourself, "I know some of those people." Maybe you're saying, "I'm one of those people, and what is it I'm doing wrong?"

Good looks do seem to carry certain people through life. We're a very vain society. One saying that comes to my mind is "God created all people equal." We all know that is not true. Some young men were born into poverty, others were born into middle class, and some were born into a privileged lifestyle.

I bring up the above analogy for a reason. By following my guide, you will be leveling the playing field. Looking, or dressing sharp has a mental effect on us, which seems most people are totally unaware of. If your clothing feels right and looks good on you, you'll start to do better work. People will start complimenting you on the way you look, which will register in your brain, and you'll start feeling better about yourself, and in turn, it will feed your physiological and/or subconscious mind. The next thing you know, you'll be producing masterpieces.

Have you ever noticed a time when you just felt sloppy? Think back to that time and what it is, or weren't doing at that time. What was the end result of what you were working on? Chances are whatever it was that you were doing, it just wasn't your best.

We all live in a highly competitive world. My book has been designed to give you an edge over the competition. Looking your best will begin to open doors for you. Being redundant, I'll say again, "Why would anyone want to shoot themselves in the foot?" Throughout the book, I'll keep repeating certain phrases. I do this for a reason and that reason is to get the information to register in your subconscious or long-term memory.

Universal Discrimination

In the late 1800s, English shop owners would post help wanted signs in their shop windows, stating, "Help Wanted." "Irish need not apply." Discrimination goes far beyond the whole color scheme of White, Black, Brown, Red, and Yellow. It actually goes back to a point where women were not treated as equals to White males as whole but fell into the same category as Black American slaves as being property of the White male. My great grandfather Claus Henry Grabau was born in Germany. He migrated to America in the late 1800s and became an American citizen and farmer in Long Island and later a farmer in Carlstadt, New Jersey. Nearing his retirement from farming, Claus Grabau needed to apply for his first Social Security card. The very thing that stood out to me was the fact that when he applied for his SSI card, he had dropped his first name of Claus and used his middle name of Henry as his first name. I have my great-grand-father's social security card in my posses-sion, my very first question was then why did my great grandfather would drop his first name and use his middle name as if it were his first name? Then it dawned upon me that he was afraid of being identified as a person from Germany. His reasoning perhaps could have been that he did not want to be affiliated as being a German. If my memory serves me to be correct, the United States of America was involved in two world wars against Germany. With that said, I recall a family rumor that at one point, my great grandfather Claus Henry Grabau wanted to go and fight the war for Germany against America. He did not, and thank, God. But I can utterly understand his position of being placed in a position of two worlds. In closing this segment on universal discrimination, I want my young readers to trace back their ancestors that had the courage to migrate to America. I want them to know and understand the barriers, challenges, poverty, and unsure futures that they were stepping into for their heirs to have a better life in the future. This includes all groups of our immigrants Polish, Italian, Irish, German, English, African, Asian, Spanish, and a world of other groups not recognized but acknowledged. They paved and paid the price for your freedom to be an American. Research their pioneering spirit and what they did for you to have the freedom and rights that you have taken for granted. My book is written to advance all teens between the ages of fourteen to thirty to help them see the pitfalls that might be holding them back from advancing in society or to propel them into the future by leveling the playing field for all be they poor, middle class, or rich.

To the privileged upper-middle class and rich that don't travel within the same circles of that of the poor or lower-middle class that are living from paycheck to paycheck just to survive, I would say sorry about your luck. If I'm leveling the playing field to a point that all are given an equal chance at succeeding in life regardless of the foundation that we were born into, then so be it. America has long stood for a country where the poor could become the rich, and the rich can become the poor. In closing this paragraph, in the past, women and slaves were treated as if they were possessions, just like cattle for the White landowner to do with as he wished. Women and slave rights were nonexistent.

With my point of view being well stated above, I'd like to share with you what I've learned over the years by paying attention to what my elders have shared with me. The history that was passed on to me and what I've retained over the years has given me the knowledge and wisdom to pass onto you what I've perceived to be truth. I know for an almost fact that from the mid nineteenth century (1850) to modern day of 2019 that women author's manuscripts were rejected for the most part by most, if not all, of the mainstream publishers of books.

Not because their works weren't note-worthy of being published but just by the mere publishing industry standards that had been established decades ago. That men write great works in writing, and women don't. This prejudgmental atti-tude forced women to take matters into their own hands, and they figured out a way to circumvent this discrimination that was being levied upon them. Cleaver as these woman authors were, they decided to either sign off as the authors under a pen name or used their initials of their first and middle names complete with the last names to make it a guess as to their gender. It worked. Most, if not all, of the current publishers at the time just assumed that they were all male writers, thus, breaking the glass ceiling in the book publishing industry that was full of prejudice at the time.

Although most of us would like to believe that in 2019 that prejudice doesn't exist any longer in the United States of America. As educated persons of all races, we simply know that is not true. My book is written to help all teens and beyond to those who are into the thirties to give them all a competitive edge. Regardless of age, race, or religion.

We all know that by law that most, if not all, in government and the private sector enterprises are prohibited from discrimination based upon age, race, gender, and religion. We also know that human resources personnel have figured out ways to circumnavigate those rules and regulations.

Genealogy in not supposed to figure into the serrano of being screened, or qualified for a position. But getting an interview with the human resources department can greatly figure into what is disclosed in your résumé. Your first name, middle name, or last name can greatly influence the HR's decision to grant you an interview or not. HR people are just like the rest of us—they're only human, and they make mistakes in judgment, just as we all do.

If your birth name strongly indicates your nationality, and you think that it might prevent you from getting to the next level because you're guilty by association, you might want to think in terms as the woman authors did in the past to break their own glass ceiling. By that I mean if your first name is Tyrone, Mohomet, or Horsey, you might think in terms of using the first and second given names as your initials with your last given name so that the HR person can't rule you out based upon your race from an interview. By that very same token, you could be knocking yourself out of the box of being interviewed for a job that is looking to meet a government standard of diversity in the workplace that mandates that they are required by law to hire a certain number of minorities to meet the status quo of diversity in the workplace. One could say that the above is, in fact, a double-edged sword. By following one rule of thinking, you may obtain an interview, and by the other rule of thinking, you may be knocking yourself out of the box for an interview. Damned if we do, damned if we don't. Life will predict what we are supposed to do and what offers we accept and what offers we reject. It is only in the very end of our lives that we see that, perhaps, we made the right choices in our lives or the wrong choices. In life, for the most part, if we've made some wrong choices, we are sometimes given the opportunity to make the right choices later in our life.

In media advertising, they use the repetition technique all the time. I think they call it the power of three. By repeating three times the same message, the viewer gets the brand, or product into the back of their mind. While shopping, you could subconsciously purchase the product. I want you to apply this same method to all that you do on presenting yourself to the world. Like I said, "We only get one chance to make the first impression." The dictionary describes the meaning of the word *first* (furst) as a noun as that which precedes all others in time, order, or importance.

Yes, I'm old school. I do remember a time when a well-dressed man would never be seen leaving the house without his hat or go to church without wearing a suit. I also remember the 1940s and fifties when teenagers would have their hair all slicked up and wore nice clothes. Boy teens of the era did so to attract girls, and it worked. I'm not advocating this book for you young men to pick up girls. However, some of my tips may result in women having a new interest in you. In the 1960s, something radically changed in the way teenagers and young men presented themselves. That era of hippies wore tie-dyed T-shirts and jeans. I'm not saying that they didn't get the girls because young women were also a part of the anti-establishment movement.

You may recall the period of greasers and hippies. It was a time when one generation was going out, and another generation was coming in. The generational identity war happens every decade. In some circles, it's called fashion. It's driven by print media, television, and today, the Internet. Each group has a need to style wardrobe to be different from the generation before them. Remember gothic?

In the 1960s, I had a cousin that refused to let go of the greaser era, and it served him well. Billy had the looks of Roger Moore from the TV series *The Saint*, which didn't hurt. Billy wouldn't be caught dead in blue jeans, or white socks, because of the community stereotype that it represented at the time. He wore dress pants, knitted Italian shirts, black socks, and black dress shoes. He had a flock of young ladies swooning over him and had his own little black book to keep track of them all. While his peers looked like they were dressed in rags.

Styles do change, and fads will come and go. In the seventies, the latest fad was leisure suits and guru jackets. Please stay away from such fads. It will only be a waste of your money. Stick to the traditional for the long haul, and you'll save money. Reconnecting with my son in the 2000s after being separated by divorce for years. I found him to be covered with tattoos and piercings. I blame part of this on the 50 percent divorce rate that we went through during the eighties and nineties where we had an absence of father figures to set examples.

One day in 2001, I had a conversation with my son. I said to him, "If you're independently wealthy, you can be as anti-establishment as you want. But if you're relying on mainstream America to support you, then there are societal rules that you must play by." I then stated that if "you're a rock star, you could be covered from head to toe in tattoos, and no one will give a rat's ass."

Again, why shoot yourself in the foot? Our military won't even consider taking you into the armed forces if you have any tattoos below the wrist, or on your neck, or face. Forget about gang-related tattoos. You're doomed. I know tattoos are the rage now but save them for the sailor, bikers, and gang members. At best, they might make it to lower middle class during their lifetime. Do you want to be rich or poor? Life is all about the choices that we make, and you certainly don't want to create any regrets along the way.

Image. Image. Image. I would like you to start paying attention to the media, advertising, and television, especially the news and weather anchors. I want you to pay attention to the way they're dressed. If need be, jot down some notes for yourself. You'll be amazed at how much you'll learn. Also, pay attention to the way lawyers, doctors, professors, congressmen, senators, and businessmen are dressed and the way they conduct themselves. You'll note that all these individuals are successful in their fields.

A lot of you are going to have a harder time making my changes than others due to the fact that you're still growing, or gaining weight. My advice to you as far as clothing purchases would be is to buy used quality clothing for now. You can resell it when you've outgrown it and apply that money to a new quality garment, which you'll own for years to come.

In the closing of my first chapter, I'd like to point out an ill-doing. An ill-doing is something that we are doing wrong. We're not even aware of it, but other people notice and are aware of it. My example is "if I'm talking to you and using my index finger to poke you in the chest as I'm explaining my point of view, I'm totally unaware of just how annoying that is to the receiving person." It isn't until my actions are pointed out to me about my ill-doing that I'm left with two options. The first would be totally ignoring the advice that I've been given and, with that risk, losing a friend. Or I can think about my action and frame in my own mind how I would feel. At that point, I can change my behavior and vow to never do it again. I state the above to make the point that my book is making you aware of the ill-doings or changes that you are going to have to make to raise your own statue in your life.

Chapter 2

Dopp Bag, Toiletries Kit, Travel Kit, or Shaving Kit

THE DOPP BAG or kit was reported to be named after a German leather goods maker named Charles Doppelt who migrated to the United States around 1900. Mr. Doppelt invented a toiletry case with the help of his nephew in 1919, and this is why we call the toiletries bag a Dopp kit today. By definition today, it is a small zippered bag that holds a man's toiletries for home or travel to keep everything that a man needs to consolidate all his grooming products in one place.

Dopp bags, although called by many names today, come in any number of sizes and materials. Although on average, they are roughly about ten inches by five inches by five inches. Materials range from nylon to leather to include canvas and waterproof canvas. The price range of these bags can be as low as less than $10 to as high as $390 for a leather coach bag. Starting out, I would suggest that you look for one on the lower end of the scale. You can always upgrade further down the line. In terms of filling your Dopp bag, I think if you start with what you already have at home, you'll save some additional money. Perhaps the next best place to purchase your toiletries inventory would be any dollar store. Drugstores are going to cost you more. Filling your bag is a very personal choice, so you need to do, or spend what is right for you. I've compiled a list below of the basic products needed with advice and suggestions on each product. I've also taken the liberty of adding some additional products that may be useful but may not be necessary. Today, we made a trip to the local Walmart, and while in the pharmacy department, my little women pointed out to me the cosmetic bags shelving unit. At first, I dismissed the idea because I said to myself, "I'm writing a book for young men." Young men need manly items, not girly stuff. Oh, what the hell. I'll take a look on one shelf. I found several brown pleather (plastic that looks like leather) top zipper bags perfect for men. The best part was the price of only $4.67 each. I opened the bag to look inside, and it appeared to be waterproof. At that price, you could buy two of them and have one for your toiletries travel Dopp bag and one for your travel shoeshine kit. Let's get started, shall we?

1. *Toothbrush.* Here, you have two choices: manual or electric. I would save the electric toothbrush for your bathroom countertop and go with the manual toothbrush for

your kit. The purpose of your kit is not only for consolidation of having all or most of your toiletries in one place but also to have it ready for travel. The marketplace is filled with manual toothbrush choices, so again, you need to find what works best for you. My manual toothbrush has small bumps on the back of the bristle head, which works to clean your cheeks in your mouth as you're brushing your teeth. You'll have to replace your manual toothbrush from time to time. Save your old toothbrush and mark it in some way to identify it from your new brush. Your old brush is the perfect tool for cleaning your combs. Just add a little shampoo to the bristles of your old toothbrush, or comb and push forward through the teeth of the comb and rinse.

2. *Toothpaste.* Toothpaste comes in about three different sizes—travel size, which is super small; medium; and regular; or full size. The travel size is good for about six to eight brushings. The medium one will last you a little bit longer. I recommend a full or regular size tube of toothpaste for a couple of reasons. On the travel size, you're paying for the packaging and, in the long run, will cost you a lot more in replacement cost. The full size or regular tube will fit into your Dopp kit and not take up that much room with notable cost savings. As far as flavor, you're on your own. Dental floss, tongue scraper, and dental pick are also a must for your toiletries kit. My stainless-steel dental pick I picked up at the local hardware store cost me about $2 ten years ago. It has served me well for the removal of plaque for the past

ten years, saving me hundreds of dollars in dental cleaning. Today, you might have to spend about $5 for the same tool but well worth the cost. Whitening strips is something else I would look into. My spouse and I attended a Moody Blues concert in Charlotte, North Carolina, and the lead singer stated that when he started out in the band that his hair was yellow and his teeth were white. Now his hair is white and his teeth are yellow. No one likes bad breath. Buy your mouthwash in bulk and transfer into smaller mouthwash containers for your kit, and you'll save additional money.

3. *Combs.* Hair texture varies widely. In fact, some men can't use a comb but must use a brush, or pick. Try to keep the combs, brushes, and picks on the smaller size because they will need to fit into your kit.

On the combs, try to buy the soft, flexible plastic ones. You should have one in your kit and one that you carry in your back pocket. The hard plastic ones break in half when you sit down, just like the screen of your smart phone. The flexible ones last a lifetime. Basic color is black for men, and they're not at all that expensive. Since we're on the subject of combs, let me make mention about hair. Keeping your hair on the shorter side is easier to maintain and creates the image of a police officer, or someone that is, or who has served in the armed forces, thus, the image of authority, and we are going for image, aren't we? Remember, first impression is perhaps 90 percent visual and a lasting one. We only get one shot at making that first impression, so let's make it our best.

4. *Razors and blades.* For God's sake, please, stay away from those disposable razors. You know the ones I'm talking about. They come in a bag of about ten, and you can buy them for a few dollars. One brand that comes to mind is BiC. If you feel that you must, just use them once and toss them after one shave. You're not going to save thousands of dollars by trying to squeeze ten shaves from one of these cheap razors. Don't waste your time or money. What comes to my mind again is manual versus electric razors. You should buy a really good quality electric razor with a trimmer. I suggest searching the Internet or eBay for the best deal. Like the electric toothbrush, the electric razor is perfect for the home bathroom but not something that you will want to cram into your Dopp kit.

However, if you just feel that you can't leave home without it, and you have to travel, you can always put them into your checked baggage for your flight. I've never felt comfortable enough to even try a straight razor. They had their heyday, but it became time to move forward. The double-edged safety razor made its debut and is still available today. This product will save you money over the three and five cartridge razors of today. If the double-edged safety appeals to you, they are still available as used on eBay, but stay away from the China knockoffs. They are garbage. Purchase a classic offered from Dad or Granddad. Bearing all that I've stated above, it seems for now, we're stuck with the cartridge razors for the closest shaves, which is going to cost us an arm and a leg. I guess you could look into some of those shave clubs offering so-called deals. As far as shaving creams, I think there are a number of them on the market. I've always stuck with a compressed can of Barbasol shave cream, and after fifty-five years, it hasn't failed me yet. Kind of bulky for putting into your Dopp kit. Roughing it a bar of soap can be lathered up into a shaving cream in a pinch.

Although I've never tried any of the hair removal products like Nair, it might be something to entertain.

5. *Nail clippers.* Two sizes: fingernails and toenails. Stainless steel. They won't rust even in the most humid of climates and chrome plated. Low-cost item and, for some of you, a must for your kit. Admittedly, I'm perhaps the worst person to be offering advice on this subject mainly because I don't practice

what I preach. I'm a nail-biter on my fingernails and that works for me well. Not recommended. The toenails. I discovered that if one were to clip the fingernails or the toenails, they can become harder than nails. What has worked for me over the past fifty years is biting my fingernails and using a pocket-knife to peel back my toenails. By my using the pocketknife, I discovered that my toenails remain on the softer side, and I'm able to trim them so that they never cause a problem, unless I trim them too short, but it's short-lived. I had an uncle that used to clip his toenails with clippers all his life. Toward his end, his toenails became so hard that it would almost take a pair of pruning shears to get them cut. In addition, my uncle went through so many pairs of socks because his toenails were so hard that they always ripped holes into his socks at the toes. I've never had to replace socks due to holes in my socks due to my toenails.

6. *Nose/ear hair clippers.* Although a tool required for some of you, I haven't found a need for myself. Nose hair is a filter to filter out the containments of what we are taking into our system or lungs. I've never owned a pair of nose or ear clippers due to the fact that I've never had to deal with the issue of ear hair and that I pull the hairs by the roots of the hair that grows in my nose. You'll have to decide what works best for you.

7. *Deodorant.* Let's face it. No one likes the unpleasant smell of anyone who reeks of body order. This is another market area that is flooded with products, and you'll have to find the best protection that works for you. Just a little tid-

bit of historical information for you about the how and why flowers and the bridal bouquet came to be at weddings. Early on, the founding of America's hygiene was not on the top of our list, but survival was. The reason, according to history, of the bridal bouquet was to mask the smell of the bride. Today, more and more women are becoming the corporate leaders, the CEOs of corporate America. For the most part, one thing hasn't changed that much. I'll call these people the gatekeepers for those at the top. The girl Fridays, administrative administers and, in the old days, the secretary. So if you're looking for any type of an edge to perhaps getting that interview for that great new job, I'm going to suggest baby powder, or also known as talc, or talcum powder. Studies have been made upon the effects that baby power or talcum powder has upon women. It has a mystical effect on babies, which conjures up a maternal subconscious instinct in women that says you are a prime candidate of a mate. This may get you past the gatekeeper but might not pull you any weight with the CEO, for here, it is now reliant upon your knowledge of the company, your past experience, and what it is that you have to offer above and beyond your competing peers.

8. *Cologne.* This product also has a flooded market with hundreds of competitive choices and not to mention price ranges. Chances are if you buy cheap in this area, you'll get a cheap product. The better colognes are oil based, just like in woman's perfumes. The sent will last a lot longer than the cheaper alcohol-based products.

My suggestion would be that you purchase a couple of small bottles and run an experiment with the woman in your life, like your mom, sister, or female friend. Ask them if they would like to participate in a blind smell test with a scoring of 1 to 10 with 1 being the least pleasant and 10 being the most pleasant of cologne smell on your body. Apply a sample on one wrist and have them close their eyes and ask them to rate. Then on your other wrist, run the same test again. Different colognes, like different perfumes, respond uniquely different on different people. This is due in part to the chemical makeup of our bodies and is based on the type of diet and beverages that we take in on a regular basis. Once you've narrowed down the best cologne that gets you the most phases, then stick with that brand and make it your signature trademark smell that everyone will know you by.

9. *Hair tonics.* If you have dry hair, you may want to consider using a hair tonic. But let's not overdo it. Like the promotional advertisement from the 1950s used to say about Brylcreem, "Brylcreem, a little dab will do you. Use a little more, and all the girls will pursue you." A product my uncle George used from the 1930s–1960. Just remember less is more. We don't want to look like we're a grease monkey that just stepped out of the garage. In my day in 1960s, the product of choice was Score. The issue I had with this product was that if I got caught out in the rain, the product would drip down my face and into my eyes, and I'd get that burning sensation in my eyes. Times do change, and the

dry look in hair became popular, so I dropped the Score hair cream.

10. *First aid kit.* Simply put, your first aid kit should start with a simple small Ziplock sandwich bag, and the contents should include not more than a dozen cotton Q-tips, a dozen Band-Aids, a small tube of a triple antibiotic cream, a dozen aspirin, a dozen ibuprofen for pain, and a dozen allergy relief tablets if you suffer from airborne allergies. Anything else that you might need can be obtained from any local pharmacy.

11. *Products for acne, pimples black-heads, and zits.* For the younger generation of my readers who may be currently suffering from the above. It appears that markedly, we have had more advice than we can handle on this subject matter from the media. At this point in our lives, we are changing from

teens to adults. What we consume as teens of pizzas, greasy burgers, french fries, and chips can affect the above over amounts of fats and oils that are required by our bodies. Our bodies are well equipped to accept what is needed in regard of minerals, vitamins, and fibers and to expel what is not needed. Therefore, our bodies will expel any excess fats or oils in the form of acne. I would caution my young teen friends not to try to pop pimples to remove the excess fat deposited upon your face. Squeezing pimples will cause the skin to puncture a larger hole in the skin, making what is called pot marks. Instead, I would suggest a hot-water facecloth to draw out the excess oils. Some of us have inherently oily skin from our ancestral genes, and as a teen, we look at this as a curse, but as we age, we discover that this trait is actually a blessing in disguise that helps us to look younger than our true age.

12. *Moisturizer and sunscreen.* The sun can cause great damage to our skin. The worst-case scenario would be skin cancer, which can be addressed by frequent visits to a dermatologist, but no one would want to go through this process later in life if it can be avoided. So please use sunscreen and moistures to help protect your skin. You'll thank me when you're older.

13. *Additional items.* Dopp bag additional items that you may want to include would be an extra cell/smartphone charger, some extra cash, a debit/credit card, spare keys, eye drops, ChapStick, breath mints, chewing gum, extra pens, and safety pins. Add the extra items that are going to address your needs.

14. *Haircuts.* I incorporate hair-cuts into this chapter of hygiene because it falls into the 90 percent range of the first impression being visual that other people will use to judge you and form an opinion of who you are and what you're about all within the first sixty seconds of meeting you. This is why the cut of your hair is so important. Adding to that, different cuts of hair do tend to send their own message. Some people can tell if you're right-handed, or left-handed by simply taking notice to the way that you part your hair. A crew-cut or flattop haircut can be inter-preted on the negative side of one being associated with skinheads or, on the positive side, of being associated with the military or law enforcement. It is the rest of your attire that fills in the blanks in the area of processing. Shorter hair is

easier to maintain than longer hair, which for young men can offer an advantage. Parting of one's hair is left, right, and center. The center part can give the man a wings look to the front of his hairline. It presents a pleasing look but can also date someone to the 1800s of the days of the barbershop quartet. The comb-over just doesn't work in any case. It's blatantly apparent that you're going bald. So don't try to hide the fact but embrace it by getting the shortest cut available. Besides that, it appears that the bald look is currently the new in look. Long hair on men was the now look of the sixties and seventies, but it also seems to have faded away. Long hair with a short center ponytail seems to send a message of an artist, or perhaps a musician. Now that I've pointed out my take on haircuts, all you have to do is see what works the best for you.

Back in the old days, as they say, it used to be that men and boys, or fathers and their sons went to the barbershops, and women went to hair salons to get their haircuts and perms. Communities supporting their local barbershops found that it doubled as a community meeting place of neighbors and friends. Patrons could learn of the latest news going on within their community.

National chains of hairdressers are changing all that by offering to cut both men, women, and children's hair. In some areas of our country, it's getting harder to find a barbershop.

One year when I was working for a living, I was sent to a community for several weeks by my agency. One Saturday that I had off from work, I decided that I needed a haircut. I couldn't find a barbershop, so I headed out to the local mall to get one.

The issue that I ran into as I went from hair salon to hair salon was that each of these businesses was asking me if I had an appointment. I promptly told them that I don't do appointments for a haircut. After my third establishment, I finally found a Supercuts, which is a salon chain with 2,802 locations nationwide. They told me that I didn't need an appointment to get my haircut and so that is where I got it cut. I mention that short story for a reason. We as consumers have what I call the power of the purse, or in men's terms, the power of the wallet. We get to decide who will get our money for goods and services and not the business. If we fold by letting the businesses make and set the rules, then we can all look forward to having to make appointments for just about everything and also have to put up with bad service as well. We control the power of the cash and who will get it and who will not. An old saying is "if you ignore your rights, they will simply go away."

Another example of this was that several banks in the suburbs of Washington, DC, had decided that they were going to charge their existing customers a monthly fee for not using their debit cards. The vast majority of the customers started closing out their accounts and opening accounts with other banks that were not trying to impose this fee. As a result, all the banks in the area that were trying to impose this fee upon their customers rescinded their new policy.

Since it's becoming harder to find a barbershop, I've decided to list below a few of the over twenty-five national haircutting establishments with some useful information about them for your convenience.

- *Great Clips.* This national chain of unisex haircutters was established in the early 1980s in Minnesota. They are open seven days a week, and no appointment is needed. They now offer an online check-in to be added to the waitlist. Because I live a few city blocks away from the Great Clips that I frequent, I just do the walk-in. I have noticed that the staff do take the online check-in customers prior to the walk-in customers. Great Clips has over four thousand locations nationally in the United States and Canada. They offer no-frills low-priced haircuts, eyebrow trimming included with the cut. Other upgrades are available at modest additional cost.

- *Supercuts.* This national chain of unisex haircutters was established in the mid-1970s. They offer no appointment required salons that also offer an online check-in list to reduce the waiting time. They offer men, women, and kids haircuts, color services, and waxing. Also offered is a hot towel refresher after your haircut. This treatment will remove the itchy and stray hairs from your face and neck leaving you feeling clean, refreshed, and sharp. I don't know if this service is included with the haircut or if it is an extra paid-for service. Supercuts have 2,802 locations and, at last count, operated 149 of them outside the United States.

- *Sport Clips.* This national chain founded in 1993 of haircutter salons looked to fill a gap in the market for men and boys' haircuts. Sport Clips has about 1,600 locations nationally and is located in all fifty states. Sport Clips also offers an online check-in waitlist. As the name suggests, the main theme of all their stores is to bring men and boys in contact with the sports world. I have visited my local Sport Clips location in Indian Trail, North Carolina.

I found that their varsity haircuts are in compliance with pricing of their competitors and the fair market value of the cost of a regular haircut in the geographical area that they have established a franchise and service.

If you, the consumer, are looking beyond the normal haircut that most men seek, I would strongly suggest that you look into a Sports Clips in your area for the full men's facial and hair treatment. The MVP (most valuable player) is a program offered as a superior upgrade to just the normal haircut. Although this service cost is twice the cost of a regular haircut. It includes the haircut, eyebrow trim cut, hot towel facial, massage chair, hair wash, and neck/shoulder massage. All included in one price. Additionally, offered at no additional charge with the MVP program is the free neck and hair trimming in between your regular or MVP haircuts.

Although other barbershops and perhaps some other national chains of haircutters may offer the same, or similar services. Sports Clips prides itself as being the leader in terms of offering to boys and men the complete refreshing message and haircutting experience.

Chapter 3

The Shoeshine Kit

IT COULD BE that you already own a shoeshine box, but if not, don't worry because I have several low-cost suggestions for you. The shoeshine kit works perfectly for at-home use but not convenient for travel. For home use, a cheaper shoeshine kit is a simple woven basket, which can be purchased at any thrift store for a few dollars. What can work for you is the small cloth bag that comes when you're buying a really nice pair of shoes. These bags come with a drawstring and will easily hold your shoe polish, dauber, and shoe brush. Another idea is the clear zippered bag that comes with the buying of sheets or pillowcases.

Again, these are free, and they serve as fine repurposing items instead of them going into the landfill. Below, I'm listing products to include into your travel shoeshine bag along with suggestions of the care of those items.

- *Shoe polish/cream/paste.* Keep it simple. Narrow it down to one small can, or jar of black. Black shoe polish perhaps being the most common. Brown and reddish brown are the second most popular colors of shoe polish, but it all depends upon your shoe colors. I've called the can of shoe polish a paste when, in fact, it's a wax and can dry out over time. One trick I learned in the military was to hold a lit cigarette lighter under the tin to melt the wax in a more uniform manner. I also carry a small tin of neutral shoe polish because it works on any colored shoe.

- *Dauber.* The dauber is used to apply the shoe polish from the can/jar your shoes. It's a short six-inch-long brush. The cheaper dauber will have plastic bristles, and the better daubers are made with horsehair. I want you to learn to clean your tools when the job is done. This is a disciplined and something of value that you can carry into a number of areas of your life. If you put your dauber back into your bag, or shoebox when finished, the next time that you want to use it, the bristles will be stiff from the dried-out shoe polish left from the time before. It only takes a few minutes to clean your dauber. Apply a drop of shampoo on the bristles at the sink, rub and rinse, dry, and you're done. I stress the point of cleaning your tools because if you don't, you'll have to stop all that you're doing and clean your tool prior to going forward. It's just a time management practice that can work for you and not against you. The putty knife and paintbrush come to mind. Have you ever grabbed a putty knife to use it only to find it was covered in hard plaster from the time before? Now you have to work twice as hard to clean that tool when a simple wipe of a rag would have cleaned it in seconds. The paintbrush you might just toss into the garbage and buy a new one. That can become costly.

- *Shoe brush.* Roughly eight inches long and about two inches wide, shoe brushes are almost always made out of horsehair and used to remove the shoe polish to shine your shoes. I have one for my black shoes and another one for my brown and reddish-brown shoes. My black shoe brush is from when

I was a child making that brush about sixty years old; thus, quality never goes out of style. One thing you can almost be assured of, and that is that as time goes forward, you will pay more and get less. I've witnessed this hundreds of times throughout my life. A prime example would be metal parts that lasted a lifetime were replaced with plastic parts that fail after a few years. It's basic economics of companies that want to stay in business—adapt or perish. This is why quality always costs a little more.

- *Shoelaces.* Shoelaces almost never break when you're taking off your shoes at the end of a day. They will break when you're running late for an appointment and in a hurry. They will always break at the most inconvenient time. For a few pennies, toss a black and brown pair of shoelaces in your shoeshine bag, or your Dopp bag, just to have on hand for such emergencies.

- *Suede cleaner.* At some point, you may come to own a pair of suede shoes, a suede jacket, or coat, suede boots, and perhaps a suede urban shoulder bag to keep your paperwork in. From time to time, these items will require some cleaning. The suede cleaner comes in a small aerosol can with a brush built into the cap. The cost is less than $10 per seven-ounce can. Simply spray the item and gently brush the area., Repeat the process for larger items. Another trick is to buy a pink rubber eraser from any stationary store and use the eraser for minor scuff marks on any suede product.

- *Liquid shoe polish.* This product I don't recommend putting into your soft travel shoeshine kit due to the fact that it could leak and make more of a mess than any-one would want to address. Great for your home shoeshine box/kit. One product in this group is Kiwi heel and sole edge dressing for making and keeping your shoes looking new. In a pinch and per-haps a worthwhile item to include in your travel shoeshine kit is a broad-tipped or chisel-tipped per-manent black marker to address heels and soles of your shoes while out on business.

- *Soft cloth.* This item is used to wipe off dusty shoes and if you're going for that military look of the spit shine. Spit shine involves using your spit with the wax shoe polish and working up in circu-lar motions a few layers of wax to bring your shoes to that patent leather look of shine.

Chapter 4

Your Space or Your Place: Organization

IN THIS CHAPTER, we're going to look at ways to organize your clothing, shoes, suits, jackets, ties, and accessories in a meaningful way of a place for everything and everything in its place. Some of you may be familiar with the term California closet, and most men know that the women in our lives take up the biggest closet spaces like the walk-in closet. While we men are left with the scraps as far as closet space is concerned.

In order to have a California closet, you'll need to have the space in your home (if you own) and, if not handy with tools and materials, a very hefty bank account. California closets can take up space of a twelve-feet-by-twelve-feet spare bedroom, or larger, and the cost can run $6,000 and up. Basically, a California closet is a built-in shelving, dresser drawer system, open-space hanging area with mirrors, recessed lighting, and literally becomes a showcase of your wardrobe.

I, having some basic carpentry skills, decided one winter in Silver Spring, Maryland, to take on the project of my own California closet room. I took a twelve-feet-by-twelve-feet spare bedroom and spent $700 and seven weeks to complete that project. I had brought back from West Virginia a five-foot mahogany dresser left at one of my properties and the four drawers from an armoire that was falling apart. I also found a nice ornate wood-framed four feet by five feet mirror. When my girl wanted to replace the bathroom mirror, I took the old one and installed it above the five-foot dresser. I purchased a dozen small brass recessed lights on eBay for almost nothing and then I headed over to Home Depot to buy three-fourth-inch finished plywood, one-eighth-inch plywood, ribbed molding, crown molding, and a gallon of mahogany wood stain. I also purchased a bundle of two inches diameter by four-foot bamboo poles and some green felt to line the drawers. I also took a double-mahogany six-foot bookcase and repurposed it by tilting the shelving to hold my thirty pairs of shoes that I now owned. This project took me seven weeks because I was working on it after my full-time day job and on weekends. When finished with the Oriental rug, it looked like $8,000 California closet. All I can say is that it came out so well that I even surprised myself, and when I retired, I think it played a big factor in selling the house. I'd be willing to bet that that room increased the value of the home by $10,000—not bad for a $700 investment. In 2015, that house sold for $400,000—not too shabby for a house that was built in the 1970s. Location, location, location.

So you don't have the space or money, but maybe you have some basic tools and how to use them. I think I can help because that pile of dirty clothes in the corner of your bedroom just isn't cutting it any longer. If you feel that your space is so crammed that you can't do anything, at the very least go out and buy yourself a hamper. I suggest that you start small but dream big because dreams can become the reality. My girl says dreaming is free. One of the very first things that you need to do is to go through your inventory of clothing. I know that for some of you, it may be very hard to let go of some of your clothing, but if you want to go forward, it is going to be a must. Toss out, give away, or donate any clothing that is too small for you now, has stains, is torn, or frayed. This will greatly reduce your inventory and will make it easier to manage and organize what is good.

Your bed makes a nice table to work on for placing into piles of like garments. For example, all sweaters in one pile, pants in another pile, and shirts, dress, polo, and tees in another. I don't want you to just toss into piles. I want you to make neat folded piles, and if you're having a problem with this, ask a woman to help teach you how to fold clothes. Now that we've gotten this far, your dresser of drawers should be completely empty. If not, keep working. I want your dresser, or dressers and closet to be completely empty. Some shirts, like dress shirts, should be hung on hangers and not folded, and you might even entertain the idea of bringing them to the dry cleaners to have them starched. It will make them look new again. Now we should be ready to start loading your folded clothing back into your dresser. Start with the bottom dresser drawer. This is where you'll want to place your stack of sweaters, then your folded pants. You can reduce the volume of some of your pants by hanging them in the closet also. You can hold onto some of your old clothes because I want you to get into the habit of changing out of your good dress clothes after work, or at the end of the day and into your play clothes. You know the ones that I'm talking about: those cotton worn blue jeans and that sweatshirt that make you feel they are part of your skin. Socks, underwear, and undershirts should go into the top drawer of your dresser. Now you know where everything is located, and you won't have to hunt for what to wear.

I'm returning back to the furniture for the storage of your wardrobe. If you have the space in your bedroom, you might be able to pick up an armoire, or additional dresser of drawers from your local Habitat for Humanity for a lot less than the retail price. Think never pay retail, always buy wholesale. Oh, and by the way, you'll need a friend who owns a pickup truck. You'll need this friend with the truck for my next advice on how to build your very own California closet room, or to at least make your bedroom look like one. As wild as this may sound, it is extremely practical, and it has to do with repurposing again. Craigslist—yes, I said Craigslist—and flat-screen TVs. No, we're not looking for the flat-screen TVs, but with the flat screen TVs coming into the marketplace, it opened up the need to dispose of the entertainment center furniture. Those sometimes huge pieces of furniture that housed the big bulky old TVs, stereos, VHS recorders, and so on. They were made in oak, cherry, and mahogany styles, which ran from traditional to early American to modern. Some had glass doors, and others had wood doors and drawers. In most cases, you can pick up these nice pieces of furniture for free on Craigslist. That big open space that used to house the big old TV can now be converted into an open hanging closet for those starched dress shirts by simply going to Lowe's, or Home Depot and buying a wood pole and the closet brackets for each end. The drawer and shelving spaces can be used for storing your clothing groups. If you decide to make one wall of your bedroom using three or four of these entertainment centerpieces of furniture, then I would suggest that you stick with all the same-type wood. In other words, if you decide to go with cherry, stick with cherry. This may mean you have to pay for the next unit that you find. Here, the keyword is uniformity and not eclectic. So let's say you like the wall unit of entertainment center furniture idea as an inexpensive way to get the desired organizational function you're looking for. The final step would be to tie all the units together to look as one. Provided they are all the same height, this could be accomplished with running molding across the front faces and top of the units. If they aren't all the same height, use the lower spaces of the tops of the units to store some of your collectibles, giving the illusion that all the tops of the units are even. Oh, here is another idea for storage of your shoes if cramped for space. Place them into pairs and place them under your bed on the outside edge of the side that you get out of the bed in the morning.

Chapter 5

Your New Wardrobe

Now THAT WE'VE organized your space and disposed of the clothing that no longer works for you, we need to start upgrading your wardrobe. I'd like to start off small and show you how a few pieces of clothing can create a different look and a different meaning in the perception of others. Let me start with the dress shirt. You should own no less than seven dress shirts. Twenty would be more appropriate. Let's say you have a job in an office, and you're required to work five days a week. With just seven dress shirts, you can wear one a day and have two extras for the next week. You will also be able to change the look by changing the tie.

Oh, you might be able to stretch the dress-shirt issue with what is called casual Fridays and a compressed work schedule. Casual Fridays don't mean that you go in to work wearing your stained blue jeans and sleeveless sweatshirt. Also, tank tops and flip-flops are totally out. What it does mean for some companies is that you can ditch the jacket and tie. Chances are the company you work for, or are going to be working for has a company dress code policy in place. My nephew works for the clothing designer Ralph Lauren, the maker of the polo brand. As a condition of employment, my nephew is required to wear the polo brand during work hours. I've seen it where the company has had to put out a memorandum to remind the staff of the company's dress code policy. It seems that some people on the job for a while just forget about the dress code. If you find yourself working for a government agency, they have rules in place about not wearing any buttons, badges, or stickers pertaining to promoting any political group. Perhaps a nice pair of dress pants and maybe a turtleneck shirt. Nicely starched khakis and a starched white shirt present a very professional look and create a clean military look. In turn, it shows that you are a person with authority. My old boss used to say, "Don't dress for the job that you have. Dress for the job that you want."

It just so happens I like to wear extra heavy starched shirts from the dry cleaners. I like them because they look crisp, no wrinkles, and just present that new-shirt look. Getting back to my statement of the seven dress shirts I mentioned in the beginning of this chapter. With only seven shirts, it creates a scheduling issue with drop-off and pickup at the dry cleaners. With twenty shirts or even fourteen dress shirts, you can have one group of seven at the cleaners while you're wearing the other group of seven.

Try to pick different style dress shirts—some with button-down collars called oxfords, some with front pockets, others without. At first, I had an issue with the no front pocket on a dress shirt, but I adjusted to the fact. Remember when I said as time goes on, you'll pay more and get less. Removal of a dress shirt front pocket did save the shirt manufacturers a lot of money in materials and labor costs. Another reason why they may have eliminated it could have been that less people were smoking cigarettes and no longer the need for the storage pouch. Although it was also I nice place to hang your pen. The no-front-pocket dress shirt does create a cleaner look. At the very least, four of your shirts should be white. It just speaks business professional. On the white dress shirt, I suggest you buy a quality oxford, a nice traditional, a French cuff for wearing cuff links, and a ribbed, or pleated tuxedo shirt.

Some dress shirts cuffs are designed with two sets of buttonholes. A white starched tuxedo shirt with no tie with a light-beige single-button suit says, "I have money." Even if you don't have money, it's just the perceptional read that others form. This gives you the flexibility to wear the shirt either buttoned or with a set of cuff links. If you have blue eyes, try to get a shirt that matches them. The same holds true with green, brown, and hazel eyes. Red dress shirts speak two things: love and war. A red shirt with a satin black tie sends a separate message on its own. In cooler climates, fall and winter wearing a sweater, or sleeveless V-neck sweater can also change the look of your shirt. With the V-neck sweater, it allows just enough space for your shirt and tie to show through to create that different image. The same holds true for vests. By mixing and matching your accessories, like suspenders versus a belt, or tie change, it can change the look with the same shirt. By doing simple things with your accessories, it makes it appear that you own more clothing than you do, and you don't run the risk of other people thinking to themselves, *He wears the same old things.*

You're going to have to learn what sizes you wear. Doing this can be done in two different ways. The first is to get someone with a fabric tape measure and do it for you. The second way is to go into your current wardrobe and find a piece of clothing that fits you perfectly and look for the manufacturer's label. Not only will it give you your size, but it will also tell you what materials the garment is made of and the care of the garment, like machine washable, or dry-clean only.

Some of you may not be willing to buy or wear used clothing, and you'll pay a premium for buying new. eBay not only sells used, but they also sell new without tags and new clothing at better-than-shopping-mall prices. In any consumer purchase, you have the power to decide who or what venue is going to get your hard-earned cash. You could catch an end-of-season sale at one of the fine men's stores that might give you a better deal than eBay with the shipping cost. Like I said before, you have purchasing power, and cash is king.

Just a little story of when I was traveling for work and had the weekend off. I forget what state I was in, but it was either July or August. The store I entered was having an 80 percent off sale on sweatshirts. I picked up a half dozen of them, and when I got to the cash register for checkout, the clerk asked me why I was buying all these sweatshirts in the heat of summer. I replied because is right, and sweatshirts never go out of style. Whenever you are ready to make a purchase of a garment, always keep in mind quality, fabric, size, construction, and cost. When buying a dress shirt, try to stick with solid colors or subtle fabric patterns. Stay away from the gaudy, loud patterns, like those flowery

Hawaiian shirts, unless you just so happen to live in Hawaii.

Although I've covered the dress shirt to a certain depth, I could go on about single meddle stitching, thickness of the buttons, collarbones, and a whole host of other things. But I just don't feel that it's necessary at this time. I'd like to move onto Hollywood, California, and the liberal take on men's clothing choices and look at this time. What I'm alluding to is the Golden Globe Awards, Emmys, Oscars, and MTV Awards, also known as the red carpet awards. I know that every generation seeks to be the trendsetters and fashion statement of the newer generation and that they seek to not dress as their fathers did. Early fifties saw tight pants and suits with narrow ties. In the seventies, it was the bell-bottom pants, and in the eighties, it was the baggy pants movement. I know that they say that history repeats itself, and in the fashion world, it seems to hold true that old styles do come back in favor again. Well, if you've watched any of the red carpet awards recently, you may have noticed that the skintight suits that the male attendees are wearing look like they just stepped out of the 1950s. It also looks like they are wearing their little younger brother's suit. I've made mention in the above paragraph because I'd like to move into the category of men's pants, slacks, and suits.

It's a broad spectrum of men that are trendsetters and trend followers. Comfort and look are the two keywords I'd go with on this subject matter. I think that taking the middle ground is your safest bet. By that, I mean the tailored look—not too baggy and not too tight that you have to worry about splitting your pants at the seams. So a straight leg cut might be your best choice. In dress slacks, the old words were cuffed slacks, or the continental look (no cuffs). I own both, but to simplify, I'd go with the continental no-cuff look. Just as with the dress shirt, pockets matter. In fact, the more pockets that are incorporated into the pants/slacks, or suits, then the better quality the slacks, or suit. The best pair of slacks or suit should have five pockets. Cheaper suits only have three pockets. Buy cheap, you get cheap. I like to carry my wallet in my rear left pocket, even though I'm a right-handed man. My rear right pocket is for my comb and handkerchief. My left front pocket is for my keys, lighters, and pocketknives. My right front pocket is for my billfold and pocket change.

I rarely use my change pocket, but it's nice to have that available to me should I have a need for it. The reason that I don't use my change, or watch pocket for back in the day when men had pocket watches is that I don't like to carry change. I have an old earthenware jug that I deposit my change into every day. It's a nice savings method that can net you $300 to $700 after several years of filling it. It can also be used as a funding source for upgrading your wardrobe.

Dress slacks can be broken down into two categories: dress and casual. The causal group would be khakis, corduroys, cargo pants, and blue jeans. A nice pair of blue jeans with a nice starched white shirt with a corduroy jacket makes a nice presentation. Add suede or leather elbow patches, and you've upped your game. Khakis worn with a white or blue shirt with a blue blazer also makes a nice presentation. Save the cargo pants for the weekends.

Your dress slacks should be made of light wool, cotton, or cotton blend and should never be washed in the washing machine but dry cleaned. Pockets count on the quality of the garment. The more the merrier. Waist should be measured above the hip. Do not wear your slacks belted above your belly button. I had a well-dressed man at work who pointed out to me a near-retirement employee who wore his pants around his belly button. My friend said to me, "If I ever start wearing my pants like that, please shoot me." I agreed. It just looked hideous. Slack length should be tailored about one inch above your shoe heel.

Limited budget with regard to buying some suits? Two suits recommend at first. Buy one light-colored single-button suit of quality for spring and summer months. Your second suit should be a single- or double-breasted dark color, perhaps small pinstripe light wool for the fall and winter months. Four suits would be preferred: two spring and summer, one single button and one double-breasted; and two fall and winter suits, one single button and one double-breasted. You can also substitute the second suit in both cases until you can afford the additional suits by buying a sports jacket for the spring and a blazer for the fall.

Since I'm on the subject of suits, I have a true story about used three-piece light-wool dark-blue pinstriped suit made by the French designer Yves Saint Laurent that I purchased from the Saint Agnes Church thrift shop in Atlantic Highlands, New Jersey, for $35. The cost of this suit was from $300 to $400 new. I made this purchase when I was twenty-seven years young, and it served me well for twenty years. That abruptly came to an end one year when I made a seriously fatal mistake of tossing my suit slacks into the washing machine and dryer. When they say dry clean only, they mean it. I don't know if this holds true today, but in the past, a really good suit came with two pairs of slacks. Count the buttons on the sleeves of your new suit purchases. This is another barometer to gauge the quality of your suit purchase. Cheaper suits and sports jackets basically have two buttons on the sleeves. Better quality suits will have three buttons sewn on the end of the suit sleeves. Finer or best-quality suits will always have four buttons sewn to the sleeves of the suit.

Middletown, New Jersey, 1984, I was driving from Red Bank, New Jersey, to home in Atlantic Highlands, New Jersey, one night and decided to take the back roads. I turned onto Navesink River Road off Route 35 in Middletown Township, which has a steep decline to the road. Even if you were doing the speed limit, you will go over the speed limit by the sheer weight of your vehicle and the gravitational pull. At the bottom of this decline, the Middletown Township had set up a speed trap, which should be illegal. I got pulled over for speeding and was cited for not having auto insurance. Court date came, and I donned a suit and tie to show respect for the court system. I knew at the time that I was in the wrong because I did not have auto insurance at that time. I did secure auto insurance prior to going to court. I arrived at the court to see about thirty other people had also been caught in this sting operation. I sat, watch, and waited for my turn to appear before the judge. I witnessed the judge slam one person after the other with $250 fines, court costs, and insurance surcharges. I also noticed that none of the other defendants wore a suit. I have a habit of saving all my vehicle registrations and past proof of insurance cards in my glove box. I had grabbed the wad of paperwork from my glovebox to bring to court. After the fifteenth person to appear before the judge, it was now my turn. I addressed the court with respect stating that I've always had insurance and that it was an oversight on my part that I didn't have insurance at the time. Just as I finished my statement to the judge, the prosecuting attorney came to my defense stating that "they wanted to drop the charges to a lesser charge of not having a current auto insurance card with me at the time." The judge asked me if I currently I had auto insurance now, and I replied yes and showed proof. The judge then stated a fifteen-dollar fine and ten-dollar court cost, which I paid on my way out of the court.

Back then, I knew I was in the wrong. Funds were tight, and it was either pay the natural gas bill to keep the home heated or pay my auto insurance. I made the choice to pay the gas bill to keep the home warm. If I didn't don the suit showing respect for the court and show a slew of paperwork to support my claims, I, too, would have been slammed with outrageous fines and insurance surcharges. My point being that the clothing that we wear is an extension of who we represent ourselves to be. If we do it properly, our clothing will do the speaking for us. The perception of others can and will either work for us, or against us depending upon the presentation that delivers.

In the late nineties, I was going through my first divorce and had to attend a child support hearing at the county courthouse in Freehold, New Jersey. Even though I wasn't divorced yet but was separated. I donned the best suit I owned at the time. In fact, it was my only suit at

0

the time. I then headed off to court. Back in those days, the attaché case was the chosen form for carrying your paperwork long before the urban shoulder bag came into play. As I'm standing in line, waiting to go into this tiny little office that had a folding table and four folding chairs, I heard someone behind me say, "I didn't know that we were supposed to bring our lawyer." I briefly looked back and noticed that I was the only person in the line that was wearing a suit. So I knew that they were, in fact, talking about me. When it was my turn to enter the office, I sat down in one of the folding chairs across from the folding table and placed my attaché case on the other folding chair, and with both thumbs on the combination latch releases, I simultaneously released the latches. I then looked up at the two women on the other side of the folding table and, by the look on their faces, could tell they were worried. Shuffling through some paperwork and with cracked voices, they said, "Oh.

Oh, this is still in process. You may go." It was like the fear of God himself had fallen upon them. I think they also thought I was a lawyer, and I'm sorry if I may have intimidated them.

Different suit. Fast forward to 2013 in West Virginia. I had to attend a court for someone that had stolen from me. While waiting in the hallway waiting area, two separate people came up to me and asked me if I was an attorney. You don't have to speak a word, people just naturally form their own opinions of whom, or what the best-dressed man is all about. I call it leveling the playing field.

Chapter 6

The Bargain Locations

IN THIS CHAPTER, you'll learn how to become a hunter. That is the hunter of the deals and steals of buying clothing, garments, shoes, and accessories. Bargain clothing deals abound everywhere. You just need to learn how to seek them out. Buying off-season is a great way to start. The trick is to find the stores that don't remove the seasonal merchandise and store it in a warehouse for the next season. Check the sales circulars for deals. Check out the discount department stores, but you need to be careful of what you're buying. Remember, buy cheap, you get cheap, but if you read the labels and thoroughly inspect your purchase, you may find a quality garment at a greatly reduced price. Now that's a bargain. As well as the chain department stores, there are the thrift stores, Goodwill, eBay, Craigslist, and the Internet. The Internet as a whole allows you to go shopping without leaving your home and can open up doors to shops in other towns, counties, states, and countries that would be next to impossible for you to get to if looking to go to that store's brick-and-mortar location.

The disadvantage to buying online is that you will not be able personally inspect the item for its quality. Another disadvantage to buying online, and this applies to buying from foreign countries, is the size labeling system. I think there are conversion table programs online to do the size conversion for you.

It seems that I've gone a little off-track of the wardrobe subject matter that I was talking about. That is because I was aware of a certain amount of knowledge that I had but just wanted to verify that what I was going to dispense was in fact the truth. I started by researching alpaca, which I knew came from Peru and South America. When I visited Peru in 1996, one of the many items that I purchased was an alpaca sweater. Some twenty years later, a coworker was going back to Peru to visit her parents. I gave her $100 and asked her to pick me up some sweaters. She returned with three sweaters that I still own today. They are now about ten years old. I must admit I didn't research alpaca on my trip, or when I asked my coworker to buy some alpaca sweater on my behalf. Since then, I've learned that true alpaca is cool to the touch and soft as a baby. Fakes are out there of blends of materials, and there is much to learn prior to purchasing. The old saying goes, "If it seems too good to be true, it isn't true." I'm happy with all my alpaca sweater purchases, although I don't think that they are 100 percent alpaca based upon the knowledge that I've just obtained. I'll cover more on this subject matter when I get to chapter 7 on educating yourself. Life is certainly a learning process, and from time to time, it can certainly enlighten the best of us.

From alpaca, I decided to research wool. My past knowledge was screaming out Irish wools, but I discounted that voice and asked the Internet who was the largest producer of wool in the world. The answer that I came up with, which was surprising to me, was Australia. I figured if I'm going to talk the talk, I need to be able to walk the walk. It turns out that Australia is the world leader in wool production. I discovered that Australia has seventy million sheep grazing the countryside. This makes Australia the world's major producer of wool controlling 25 percent of the world market. According to the current data of 2015, Australia produced 478,492 tons of wool. High-quality wools (merino) are used to produce clothing. Lower grades of wool are used to produce blankets, carpets, and upholstery. Coming in second place is China. So it only makes common sense that if you are looking for the best value and the best price for a 100 percent wool jacket, or suit that you would look for clothing manufacturers in Australia. Although this may make perfectly common sense, it might not hold true on a finished garment, like a jacket or suit. So I would encourage you to seek out the best product at the least cost regardless of what country controls the raw materials.

My research then led me to investigate Egyptian cotton. I already knew that the best bedsheets were made of Egyptian cotton from what I had read, and it was the thread count of one thousand that made the difference from any other manufacturer. So I took a gamble and researched on the Internet men's shirts made from Egyptian cotton. I found that the top clothing designer Joseph Abboud used one thousand thread count in the manufacture of his men's shirts. So here we had it, the finest cloth material used to manufacture the finest of men's shirts. Quality, quality, quality. As I continued with my search, I came upon a men's warehouse website offering a shirt designed by Joseph Abboud made of 100 percent Egyptian cotton with a front pocket and French cuffs in lavender regularly priced at $104.99 on sale at clearance for $9.99. My girlfriend, knowing a bargain when she sees it, encouraged me to make the purchase as my future birthday present. My Donna allowed me $30 as my birthday gift and encouraged me to place an order. I'm going to break from this for a second, but I'll get back to you in a second. I have a very important message to deliver to you.

The whole and sole purpose of me teaching you to buy right is to teach you to save money. By saving money, it places you in a position to be able to make a move on an opportunity for growth without having to be put into a position that you have to borrow money. The rich buy assets that can make them additional money. The poor buy liabilities, which cause them to lose money. The poor are unable to make the larger purchases of assets that can make them more money because they have spent their money on the instant gratification syndrome of I have money. "Look at me." I can afford to purchase what I want while the rich hold onto their money until the greatest opportunity for growth and profit can be made from their investment of their money. With that said, I'll continue. The poor seek to obtain instant gratification of their current wealth by buying liabilities. The middle class and the rich are interested in buying assets that will grow and make them more money.

Learn to become frugal with your money and understand the power of it and how it works for you. Those individuals who don't have any money are quick to call frugal individuals as cheap, and you might even notice that they are the first ones to blame the rich for their problems. If I can teach you to spend less on your wardrobe and become a saver of money, it will place you into a position of power. The poor and some middle-class people seek instant gratification. What I mean by that is that when they have some money, they feel compelled to go out and spend it. In part, they do this to show other people that they have disposable income, even if they don't. But they shop anyway because in the eyes of the other customers in the store, or impressing their friends by showing off what they just bought makes them feel good. Then when the true bargain deal comes along, they must pass up the opportunity because they don't have the cash, or credit to move on it. The rich can avail themselves of a great buy because they saved their funds and have great credit. So when that super deal comes along, they can seize the moment and close the deal. That kind of transaction is what makes the rich feel good.

So seeing the opportunity to purchase high-quality new shirts at a fraction of the cost, I proceeded with my online order.

The issue that I ran into was that the clearance items are limited based upon size and so I was not able to avail myself of all the discounted quality shirts. Although this clearance of quality shirts didn't fully work for me, that doesn't mean that it won't work for you. In the end, I purchased two quality shirts for a total cost of $24.98 plus tax $2.23 and shipping $8 for a total cost of $35.21 delivered to my doorstep. As opposed to spending $204.98 plus tax and shipping, thus, saving me over $169.77 if I hadn't bargained shopped. In the long run, I probably saved myself over $250 to own the same two shirts. Thus, I think that I've proven my point that sometimes it is better to search the major department chains of the finer men's stores clearance section online than it would be to search eBay online, or to visit a brick-and-mortar discount department store.

Flea markets are another great source for buying clothing at bargain prices. The pitfall will be that you're less likely to find high-quality garments there unless they're used. You could run into someone who was of means that happened to fall upon hard times, and they are just looking to get rid of some excess high-quality goods to raise a few dollars. You're most likely to find new packaged underwear, socks, and T-shirts at lower-than-department-store prices. You'll experience a cost savings, although it won't be a great one. But money saved is still money saved.

Chapter 7

Educating Yourself

My book is just the tip of the iceberg for you. Yes, it will enlighten and educate you, but this book is designed to pique your interest to a mind-altering state of mind that I want to reach your subconscious to the point that your way of thinking becomes reactionary to the point of where you don't have to think about quality, bargains, or saving money but that it just comes naturally to you. The old proverb says, "Give a man a fish, and he will eat for a day. Teach a man how to fish, and he will eat for a lifetime." Although the saying's origin is in question, the point I'm driving to is that if I tell you all that I know in this book, it's like giving you a fish, but if you take my advice as a way of life, it is as if I taught you to fish. If you take it into another context, what I'm trying to teach you is to fish—to fish for the greatest sales, the lowest prices, and the best quality, or bang for your buck.

Perhaps I was thirty years old at the time. I lived in a coastal town called Atlantic Highlands, New Jersey. The town was sort of broken up into two distinct districts. The main street was known as First Avenue and ran from the highway called Route 36 to the municipal harbor. The harbor became known as the million-dollar harbor of Atlantic Highlands. The docks held close to a hundred expensive powerboats, and off the docks was a mooring area for twenty-four feet to forty feet high-end very expensive sailing yachts. Coming off the highway to the left of First Avenue was known as the lowlands. It was level and filled with modest- to medium-priced homes. To the right of First Avenue and

Scenic Route, which was an uphill road that climbed the bluff. The bluff overlooked the bay, harbor, and marina. This side of town had very expensive homes. At the time, $200,000 to $500,000 homes dotted the hillside. One never needed to ask where the wealthy part of town was. All one had to do was look. I purchased my second home on the bluff off Scenic Route. One day while I was working in my side yard, I met a wealthy sailor neighbor who lived on Scenic Route. He was out for a summer day walk. We chatted up a conversation, just general talk I can't remember about what. But the subject changed to him complimenting me on how much work I had done to improve my house. I told him that I didn't have a lot of money and that if I was going to be a homeowner that I needed to know as much as I could learn about plumbing, electrical, painting, carpentry, tile, and yard work, or I was going to have to pay someone else to do it. My sailboat-owning neighbor then said to me, pointing to his head, stated, "What I don't have up here, I have to take out of here," as he pointed to his right front pants pocket. Meaning that he was going to have to pull the cash out of his own pocket to pay for what he did not process in his own mind. Nor did he have the tools, wisdom, knowledge, or power to execute to his own benefit, hence, a twofold situation? One can learn the skills needed to confront all handyman skills with tools to accomplish almost any home repair need, or have the skills of generating money to pay for the skills of others to get the same job completed. I never forgot that life lesson, and it scores among the top ten lessons that I received over the years.

Knowledge and education are powers that can be applied to so many different areas and situations in your life that can carry you up the ladder of success. Research, research, research. You have a very distinct advantage today over me when it comes to researching something or educating yourself. When I was growing up, it was the library, or if you were lucky enough to own a set of books called the encyclopedia, then one could research, or look up a subject matter. Other than that, you read the newspaper, books, or listened to your elders who could impart fact or fiction upon you. Your very distinct advantage is the Internet. You're only limited by your own imagination in terms of what you want to learn or get the real facts on. Just take the subject on wool that I mentioned earlier. If I didn't research the subject, I would never have learned that Australia was the largest world producer of wool, and it makes sense that if you're looking to get the best deal on a wool product, you would want to search the place where they have an abundance of the raw material. Sometimes we can't learn by research. Sometimes we have to learn by trial and error. Take the barbecue backyard grill for example. I've went through about a half a dozen steel barbecue grills that just kept rusting out on me. One of the first parts to rust out is the drip tray. Before I learned that although steel barbecue grills aren't that costly, replacing them over time can add up to a pretty penny, meaning several hundred dollars.

The stainless-steel barbecue will cost you a lot more on the front end, but over time, it will cost you a lot less. I found a Kirkland stainless steel grill with an oven on eBay that was in Red Bank, New Jersey, a place I was familiar with that was listed for $300. I researched the grill and found that new was a $1,200 grill. I bid on it, and no one bid against me, so I won it. I drove from the state of Maryland to New Jersey and picked it up. Eight years later in North Carolina, I still own that grill with no issues.

Frankly, I don't care how you obtain your purchasing power knowledge prior to spending your hard-earned cash, but please do your homework prior to buying any-thing. Once you've secured the asset you've been searching for, you need to maintain it if you don't want to be forced into buying that item again. It's called preventive maintenance. If you own a car, you should know exactly what I'm preaching here. By taking care of what you own extends the life of what you own. This is why my shoe brush is sixty years old. Shoe brushes don't require a lot of care, but if you take care of what you own, it will take care of you.

In Maryland, I had a neighbor named Charles who was a scientist and was working on black holes in space. Charles was a very educated and smart man but lacked a certain amount of common sense. Charles had a fairly new power push mower that he couldn't get started. I went over to help him out with his problem, which was that the air filter was clogged beyond belief. I cleaned it, and it started right up. A few weeks later, he blew the mower up because he didn't add any oil. Charles purchased another new mower, and within a month, it was smoking, like he was on mosquito control. His son stopped him from continuing on mowing the lawn. I think Charles overcompensated and put too much oil in the mower. Charles's wife hired a lawn care company to address their yard. Was it bad luck? Or did Charles just not educate himself on the equipment he purchased?

Sy Syms Corporation (1959–2011) retailer of designer and brand name clothing coined the phrase "An educated consumer is our best customer." He might have coined that phrase because he knew that a knowable person would recognize the quality of a garment and would not mind paying a little more because the item was worth the extra money. I had a coworker named John that had worked for United Airlines who had two sayings, "It doesn't cost that much more to fly first class," and "Honesty is doing the right thing when no one is looking." John had also worked in law enforcement. There is truth in both of his sayings. I also had a boss that would say, "Live your life as if the following day was going to be printed on the front page of the New York Daily Newspaper and that you would not be embarrassed by anything it printed." Wise men. I have a saying of my own, "Some people know the price of everything but the value of nothing." I incorporate theses sayings for frame-of-mind knowledge in terms of living right. When shopping, if the clerk gives you too much change back, inform them right away and return the money. I once purchased an item in the store and paid with a ten-dollar bill. The clerk gave me change back as if I gave her one hundred dollars. I informed her, and she lifted the cash register drawer and saw that I was right. She thanked me profusely and said that if I hadn't informed her, the company would have deducted it from her paycheck. I'm teaching you how to save money and not rip people off. My teaching you the proper presentation to make does not mean that I what you to become a wolf in sheep's clothing. Let me wrap up this chapter by asking you to create a values-and-principles format in your brain that can be called upon when asked to do something that goes against what you have established as you live by rules. What I'm trying to explain here is a simple mental list of your values and principles. Your mental list, which you can visualize when needed, would simply state that you do not lie, cheat, deceive, steal, or manipulate. When approached by others who don't have a moral compass that ask you to lie for them, you can simply reply with a no and state that you have a moral compass of values and principles that you live by and that their request goes against your grain. I also embrace a more-positive section to my values and principles list of honesty, integrity, respect, and legal. In the Catholic Church, they call their list the Ten Commandments.

I had a boss once that had purchased about a half-dozen dress shirts from Sears,

Roebuck and Co. He wore these shirts for about fifteen years, and when the collars started to fray from normal wear and tear, he returned the shirts to Sears and received new shirts in their place. I thought what he had done was deceitful, and he also boasted about what he had done.

In bringing this chapter to a close. As part of your bargain hunting, I would like to leave you with two more additional quotes. "After birth, death is inevitable. Everything else is negotiable." Keep that quote in mind whenever you're negotiating with someone who tells you it can't be done. My second quote can serve you well when seeking out a true bargain. "It is the ability to recognize and seize an opportunity, which distinguishes the entrepreneur from the ordinary businessman." I can't take credit for either of these quotes because I picked them up going through life.

Chapter 8

Clothing and Cars Are Extensions of Ourselves

IN THE VERY beginning, I explained that our appearance accounts for at a very least a 90 percent perception of who we are and what we represent to others. Another saying that comes to mind is "Is it the man that makes the clothes, or is it the clothes that make the man?" Another preverbal saying is "Does art imitate life, or does life imitate art?"

So as you prepare to make your visual presentation to the world, a few things to keep in mind. Where are you going? Who are you meeting? Who will you run into?

And what is the main purpose of going out? All these questions play a very important role in terms of what you are going to wear. Naturally, you're not going to dress up in a suit and tie if you're going to the grocery store. However, you might not want to wear the blue jeans and sweatshirt because you could have a chance encounter. That chance encounter could be with the human resources person that you just met last week in an interview, and you're still waiting on the company to get back to you with regard to whether you have the job or not.

I'm not trying to make you neurotic with overdressing but that second chance meeting with the HR person could sway their second option of you and have her change her mind about hiring you. By the same token, if you have a job, and you're going to Lowe's to pick up ten bags of mulch for your landscaping at home, then why not wear the blue jeans and sweatshirt.

So prior to venturing out into the world, just take a minute to think about the whom, the what, and the where, and the happenstance encounters of whom you may meet. We may, based upon our presentation of our attire, be pleasantly surprised at the outcome that could develop by just giving a little forethought.

Think of your clothing presentation as being an extension of yourself. Well, the same holds true with the vehicle that you drive. Have you ever entered into a vehicle that was so filthy that you couldn't wait to get out of it for fear that you might catch some kind of disease? I have found myself in such vehicles with spilled soda cans, paper candy wrappers, chewing gum on the floors and seats, stained seats, dirty windows, and enough papers and junk on the dashboard, leaving you wondering how the driver could even see to drive. Oh, yes, and the smell. That visual should leave you in no doubt that the driver's clothing presentation was just as poor of an example of who and what they are all about.

Keeping your car, or truck clean doesn't require that much more additional afford on your part. Don the garden hose once a month to wash off the road dust. Keep a small trash bag on the passenger-side floor and empty when needed. Or just get into the habit of removing the garbage from your vehicle when coming back from a road trip. Once clean, the upkeep isn't rocket science. So let me ask you another question. How do you think you would feel if you had gotten all dressed up for an appointment and had to step into a filthy vehicle? Would you worry about soiling a new suit?

Chapter 9

Accessories

ACCESSORIES ARE THE gadget-type items like sunglasses, pens, pocketknives, cuff links, lighters, watches, rings, neckties, gloves, tie tacks, suspenders, necklaces, handkerchiefs, scarves, hats, belts, walking sticks, wallets, money clips, lapel pins, umbrellas, and today, urban shoulder bags. I've decided for this chapter to list each item as a separate subject and describe the item and function, materials, best places to acquire, and in some cases, a brief history of the item.

Sunglasses—sunglasses are available in a large array of styles and materials. I feel that the vast majority of them are made out of plastic, or a plastic-metal mix. Pricing on this item runs the gamut from a few dollars for a cheap pair to several hundred dollars for designer-brand names. Oakley, Ray-Ban, Maui Jim, Prada, and Gucci are just a few of the designer brands that come to mind. Buying these brands could have a serious effect on your wallet with prices ranging from $150 to $600 a pair. If you have the disposable income to afford a pair, and it's a brand you can't live without, buy them. In addition to mirrored and polarized finishes, I think you can also get scratch residence lens, or other films applied. Some people just can't buy regular sunglasses due to their eyesight and must wear prescription sunglasses. As for myself, I can't tell you how many good pairs of sunglasses I've broken, and since I don't have an eyesight issue, I just buy the low- to medium-priced pairs. If they break, I'm not out much money. I've found the Internet to be the best place to research all your sunglasses needs.

Pens, also known as writing instruments, have been around for over six thousand years. Are they going away in the future? According to some of the pen manufacturers, the answer is no. Will pens evolve into becoming something different from what we know today? The answer is yes. Like most products we are familiar with, there is an evolution that takes place. The pen itself has seen many evolutions in the past, so why should the future be any different? Already in the works, or development stages are pens that light the barrel of the pen, pens that can write in 3D, holographic pens are coming that don't require a substrate to write on because you'll be able to write in the air, and digital pens are also coming. I know that the group I'm addressing does a great amount of texting on their smart phones, and we have formats for sending electronic signatures. There will be times when a writing instrument will be required in your daily life. Promotional pens you can get for free, they are usually cheap ballpoint pens and will work in a pinch. Find a pen that you feel comfortable with in your hand and has a smooth flow of ink. Price-wise, your cost should be less than one dollar. Each person has to find the right type of pen that works for them. I started with a Sheaffer refillable fountain pen in elementary school. From there to the cartridge fountain pen to the BIC ballpoint stick pen to the Cross pen and mechanical pencil set to my current choice of gel pens. The drawback to the gel pens is that they are not refillable. On the high end of pens, I found a Mont Blanc Peggy Guggenheim Limited Edition 888 fountain pen for $8,465 on the Internet. Any pen—ballpoint, gel pen, or fountain pen—that meets your needs will do. Just make sure that it is comfortable and has a nice ink flow that you like. For now, I would keep the price down $5 to $40 at the very most should pay.

Pocketknives—carrying a pocketknife is your own personal choice. I prefer to carry several pocketknives due to the properties that I own. It seems in my case that I have a constant need to have one available to open packages, cut rope, or twine, and a whole other host of situations where I need one. Your needs may not be the same as my own. If you decide that it would be wise on your part to carry one, then I would suggest that you find a pocketknife that meets your needs. Buck knives have a fine reputation for quality and so does Schrader. They come in several blade knives and in single locking blades. Pricing can range from the low side of a few bucks to the high side of many bucks.

Another consideration is the multipurpose tool, which will consist of multiple blades and other tools like a saw, can opener, pick, file, scissors, pliers, and plumb bob, just to name a few. Gerber is perhaps one of the top-of-the-line manufacturers in this group. The Gerber comes with a webbed carrying case that attaches to your belt. Gerber is priced slightly above their computation. But their quality speaks for itself and is well worth the price, especially if you find yourself in one of the blue-collar trades like electrician, computer hardware, carpentry, or property maintenance. Prices vary depending upon brand and source of supply. Your best bet is to search the Internet for the best deal that meets your needs.

Cuff links—cuff links are only required for your finer dress shirts, the ones with the French cuffs. I'd suggest that you only own a few pair; perhaps one or two pairs of gold fill will do. I wouldn't own any more than six pairs of cuff links. Today, you can buy a tie that will come with a matching pair fabric of fabric cuff links and matching handkerchief online for under $20. I own about a dozen cuff link sets and find myself wearing an oval gold-filled pair with a brushed finish. They look the best, and I could have had them engraved with my initials. But why spoil a great look? Over time, you'll find out what works best for you.

Lighters—although, today, you might think that a lighter is an accessory that you might not need. Trust me, my friend, you will have a moment when having a lighter is going to be essential. Just try lighting a candle at that perfect moment with your best female friend and having no lighters, or matches to do so. Perhaps it's a tiki torch, firepit, or even a barbecue grill that just won't light on the electronic ignition. I know that smoking is out of favor, and most people are vaping nowadays, but some people will still enjoy a great cigar with a glass of spirits. Just imagine you're the only person at a party with a lighter. You could be the star attraction. Today, lighters are super cheap, at least the disposable ones. For less than $2, you can buy a half-dozen pack of them. The old school Zippo lighters that ran on lighter fluid can cost you from $5 to $34, depending upon where you're purchasing them from. In the

1960s butane lighters were the favorites. Today, they also have electronic lighters. You pick what works the best for you. Search the Internet to see all the available types and prices.

Watches—with smartphones posting the time on them, the younger generation might feel that they do not have any need today for a wristwatch. However, wrist-watches are not only a means of telling the time of day, or night. They have become a status symbol of your station in life in accordance with our class system. Wearing a watch today symbolizes that you are a person of means and money and perhaps that you have a great deal of disposable income. In the general scheme of things, the average person will assume that you are a person of wealth by the mere fact that you are wearing a watch, just the same as they will assume that you are wealthy if you are driving a Mercedes-Benz, or a BMW car. This doesn't mean that you have to plunk down $210,000 for a Rolex Daytona Paul

Newman 6239 watch, or a Patek Philippe 5208P001 for $1,230,000. However, you could sport an Invicta watch priced from $1,119 to $59,000 or a Relic watch for under $100. As long as you are honest, if and when someone may confront you about your watch and its cost, you'll have nothing to worry about. But if you try to deceive a knowledgeable person, you may find yourself in a very embarrassing position.

I purchased a diamond-studded watch and watchband from eBay, and it had lots of bling to it. It drew a lot of attention at work. I was always honest about the cost and where I had purchased it. The responses I always received were very positive, and no one ever gave me the impression of any negativity toward me or the watch. On occasion, I would receive advice from some of my coworkers with concerns about my safety for wearing a watch with such bling in Hyattsville, Maryland. But I never had an issue. I understood their concerns, and if I were ever confronted, the assailant could have the watch.

Rings—limit your ring wearing to no more than three rings. Less looks better than more, and too many rings looks tacky. Silver rings are less expensive than gold, or platinum rings. Today, they are also selling rings made of stainless steel, or titanium. You can find them on the Internet. Rings are also available with semiprecious and precious stones. Lots of people enjoy wearing their birthstone rings.

Wedding bands are worn on the left-hand ring finger. If you have worn a wedding band for some time, and now you're thinking of cheating on your spouse, don't think that for one moment that you can simply remove your wedding band and get over on a woman. Women are a lot smarter than most men think. They will be quick to point out to you that you are married. They base this information on the fact that where you wore your wedding band will lack a tan on your skin.

Pricing on gold rings is based upon the karat of gold contained. Pure gold is twenty-four karat and is too soft to wear as jewelry. Karat or K scale is 10K, 14K, and 18K. The higher the number, the more gold it contains. Gold is melted with other metals like copper, or nickel to increase the hardness of the jewelry. Gold also comes in different colors, like white gold, rose gold, and yellow gold. When shopping for your rings, the fit is very important. You don't want to wear a ring that is too tight, or too loose on your fingers. Your ring purchases are a personal choice, so buy something that you truly like.

Neckties—shoestring neckties seem to be favored in the Southwest. It's considered to be of the Western style for a man dressing up. Neckties are produced in narrow, medium, and wide widths. The production of the width of a necktie seems to be economically driven. One would think that wider ties would be made in good economic times and that narrow neckties would be made during bad economic times. However, I've noticed this trend to be the complete opposite. I think the rationale behind this has been in place within the rag business for many, many decades. I feel that the thinking is that during hard economic times that clothing sales are down. During hard times, it is more important to put food on the table than to go out and spend nondisposable income—your clothing. So the garment industry in making the wider neckties is a simple marketing strategy used to entice the consumer. The message being delivered is that you are now going to get more bang for your buck because the manufacturer is now adding more fabric into the making of a wider necktie. The consumer takes notice and so a new cycle of the current fashion trend is starting again. I also noticed this with the lapel's width on men's suits and the reintroduction of the double-breasted suits. With the trend set, all end garment products are produced with using more fabric material.

During better economic times, the garment industry will start producing narrower neckties. There is more money flowing in the economy, and a lot more people have disposable income. This period gives the garment industry a chance to increase their profit margin and to make up for any losses they may have incurred during the leaner days. So a new fashion trend is started of getting less fabric in the clothing that we're purchasing. You'll also start to notice that the lapels on jackets and suits will become smaller, baggy pants will be out of style, and single-button suits will be the new norm.

I used to think that the best time for buying works of art, like paintings and sculptures was during good economic times. I may be right on that assumption as far as investing. But during good times, I learned through an art collector friend of mine that the art world market isn't that hot. According to my friend, the art world market is at its hottest during bad economic times. He explained to me that during bad economic times, investors are looking for different ways to invest their money to grow as a hedge against inflation. Warren Buffett, stock market investor, has said the best time to buy stock is when everyone else is selling and the best time to sell stock is when everyone else is buying. Well, if one were to apply the same principles in the art world, then I would say buy art in a good economy and sell art in a bad economy.

Necktie fabrics are polyester, stain-resistant microfiber, silk blends, and silk. Noted as being the best is the 100 percent handmade pure silk neckties. Prices on the pure silk neckties can range from a low cost of $20 to a high price of $230 for a single necktie. The Internet is perhaps the best place to research and purchase your neckties. One site that I discovered is www.cheapneckties.com with prices ranging from $5 per tie made of the stain-resistant microfiber. Their next group of $10 and $15 ties are a blend of silk and microfiber, and their last group is $20 per tie for a 100 percent handmade pure silk tie. On eBay, you can purchase a single necktie, or you can buy them in new in tie set lots of six, twelve, or more for about $20 a set. The most expensive necktie in the world that I found will set you back $220,000 by Suashish. It's made of silk, 150 grams of gold, and 271 diamonds. Designer neckties will cost more than off the shelf neckties, and with these neckties, you're paying for the designer name and the quality of the garment.

Clip-on neckties are made for children, so you're going to have to learn to tie your own neckties. This means that you'll have to learn how to tie a half Windsor and double Windsor (also known as a full Windsor) tie knot. You may also want to learn how to tie a bowtie. I wouldn't bother because you can buy a bowtie with an adjustable strap and fastener to meet your needs without reinventing the wheel.

The assortment of necktie colors and fabric graphics are endless. The range of solid colors, stripes, polka dots, floral design, palsies, and iridescent is enough to boggle the mind, and I'm sure that I've missed some. Find the neckties and bow-ties that work best for your needs in terms of necktie width, color, pattern, and price.

Gloves—when I'm talking gloves, I'm addressing dress gloves. I thought calfskin black, or brown lined dress gloves were the best you could buy until I educated myself. Research sent me in a different direction. What I discovered was that lambskin that is cashmere-lined dress gloves offer an extremely soft outer shell with a warm lining. Addressing quality the dress gloves that I just described will cost you close to the one-hundred-dollar range. Men's dress gloves come in the outer shell in suede, deerskin, lambskin, cowhide leather, pig-skin, and goatskin. Dress gloves also have a diverse number of linings to include wool, rabbit fur, and cashmere to just name a few. The idea behind dress gloves is to have them fit snuggly and keep your hands warm. The bulky looking dress gloves take away for that refined look. Find a pair that meets your needs based upon the shells and liners that I mentioned above that fit your budget. Expect to pay $20 and up for quality dress gloves. My black dress gloves are 100 percent soft genuine leather with 66 percent wool, 31 percent nylon, and 3 percent polyester lining. They look good and keep my hands warm in winter and cost about $20.

Tie tacks—tie tacks, tie pins, and tie bars all serve the same purpose and that is to keep your straight long tie out of your soup at dinnertime. Forgive the pun on the soup at dinnertime. The true purpose of a tie tack, pin, or bar is to keep your dress tie as close to your dress shirt as possible and to prevent your tie from getting into your way as you go about your daily business on the job.

Let's say you just so happen to be an architect and you're trying to show your client the latest blueprints that you just produced on your new CAD (computer-aided design) system of some innovative design changes that are going to save your customer a great deal of money on his project. You've laid the blueprints out on your design table, and every time you lean forward to show your customer a design change that is going to save him thousands of dollars, your flopping dress tie lands directly on the spot of the blueprints that you're looking to highlight, and your tie is completely blocking the view. If you continue to have this happen to you and your client, I can almost guarantee that your client will lose interest in what you are trying to point out to him or her.

Given the above scenario and knowing that you're a smart guy, you come up with this ingenious idea of opening your second or third button on your dress shirt and immediately tucking the bulk of your hanging dress tie into your shirt and refastening the button. That worked and saved the day.

A simple tie tack, pin, or tie bar put on in the morning as you dress for the day at the office would have had you already prepared for the day. Tie tacks, pins, and bars sometimes come with buying cuff links, and the design or pattern usually matches the cuff links. Tie tacks, pins, and bars are also sold separately and come in a wide variety of materials. The most common is gold, gold filled, or gold plated, silver, or chrome plated. Although relatively inexpensive, some tie tacks can be mounted with semiprecious, or precious stones that can drive a price up. Tie tacks tend to have a small fine chain attached to the pin with a buttonhole bar on the end. The bar is designed to insert into the buttonhole directly across from where you inserted the pin into your tie. The purpose is to limit the travel the tie is going to drift away from your dress shirt.

I've researched the cost of tie tacks, tie pins, and tie bars, and I've found that most can be purchased for just a few dollars. The most expensive tie bar that I found was offered by three major department store chains and cost about $60 and didn't even include precious stones. In closing this part of tie tacks, pins, and bars for your dress ties, I would say that a number of companies will give as gifts tie bars promoting their company. An example is Atlas Screw Company giving away to their customer a tie bar with a gold-plated wood screw on the tie bar. Very tacky outside the fastener industry business.

Suspenders—suspenders do tend to make a fashion statement. Bright-colored suspenders of red, yellow, blue, green, and orange, when worn with a contrasting color shirt, are screaming, "Hey, look at me." If you're looking to stand out from the rest of the crowd and want to be the center of attention, then don a pair of suspenders. Suspenders are a relatively inexpensive accessory but do make a bold statement. Generally, less than $20 per pair of the all-purpose type that come with snap clips are adjustable in size and can be worn with any dress slacks.

They are also available on the higher end of the scale and, in place of the clip snaps, have leather tabs with buttonholes. The cost of this business-class suspenders can start as low as $34 per pair and run as high as $168 per pair. They're available in fabric, canvas, leather, and suede. This type of suspenders is designed to be worn with high-quality slacks that have buttons sewn into the waistband of the slacks. This style creates a slightly cleaner look.

Necklaces—necklaces, religious pendants, chains, and crosses all come in a variety of metals and price ranges. They are designed to be worn under your clothing or exposed. They are personal to you and have meaning to you as to why you've chosen to wear them. I would keep this item to a minimum of owning one or two.

Handkerchiefs—the handkerchief is a square piece of cloth twelve inches by twelve inches and sometimes larger made of cotton, cotton blend, silk, linen, and wool. Although most are white, it is for hygiene purposes of blowing one's nose, or for the wiping of tears. When used as an accessory to a suit jacket's top left pocket, it becomes known as a pocket square. Pocket squares sometimes come with the purchase of a dress tie of matching fabric and design pattern. Pocket squares are usually cut smaller than handkerchiefs for the suit pocket to prevent the bulk look. Wikipedia lists fourteen ways of fold patterns for the pocket square complete with the names of each fold. Pocket squares and handkerchiefs were very popular from the 1920s to the 1960s when they fell out of favor. In the 1990s, they made a comeback for the well-dressed man. Handkerchiefs and pocket squares average about one dollar each and can be bought in bulk lots, boxed sets, and individually. Online merchants offer an array of fabric material and pattern designs. eBay is the site that I'd suggest for starting your search.

Scarves—the man's scarf's main purpose is to keep the back of the neck warm or to shield the back of the neck from the sun. The man's scarf also doubles as a fashion statement of the well-dressed man. In the same category of scarves are neckerchiefs and ascots. Since neckerchiefs and ascots for men aren't as popular as a man's scarf. I've decided to just focus on man's scarves.

The true appreciation of owning a scarf and having it in your possession comes at a time when you find yourself out in the cold and the temperature is in the teens. Scarves are made of silk, cashmere, wool, linen, cotton, acrylic, angora, synthetic materials, and fabric blends. They are made in widths of six inches to fourteen inches and come in lengths from fifty inches to ninety inches. The average length is sixty inches, and they have scarf width and length charts available online for finding your perfect fit. My rule of thumb is a twelve-inch-wide scarf doubled over to create a six-inch-wide scarf, and when draped over the back of the neck, the ends of the scarf do not fall any more than four inches to five inches below the waistline. When tied, the scarf should raise to your waist. Prices range from under $10 to as high as $850 each. Designer scarves would fall on the higher end of the price scale. I recommend that the beginning buyer of scarves keep the purchases down to a quantity of four scarves. I suggest one black, brown, gray, and white in cashmere, wool, linen, and silk.

Hats—I've never been a hat person myself, but perhaps I should have been due to my height of 5'5". A dress hat can add three to four inches to your height profile and considering that the average male is 5'7" to 5'8" tall, a hat can add to your status.

Beyond the above, I've developed a very personal reason for not wearing a hat. Growing up in my teens, both my younger brother and cousin wore hats, and today, both are bald in their midsixties while I still have a full head of my blond hair with no signs of balding. I'm quite sure that bald people and the doctors in the medical field will disagree with my reasoning. The purpose of a hat is to keep the head warm and to keep the elements of weather off your head. Some hats are used to provide shade from the sun. Hair is nature's way of keeping the head warm and prevents the heat from escaping from your body.

By wearing a hat day in and day out, year after year, the heat that is generated from the body escapes through the top of the head. Heat raises. The body and mind react when the heat is trapped between the top of the head and the hat that is trapping that heat, which cannot escape. The results would be for the brain to tell the body to lose some of the hair to bring down the temperature in the head area. The process of hair loss continues every time the heat levels get too high. At a certain point, men continue to wear the hats, even indoors, to hide the fact that they are going bald, which then compounds the loss of hair. To support my theory, I ask you this question, "Have you ever seen a man balding on the sides of his head that the hat is not covering?" I'm going to guess that your answer is a resounding *no*.

Okay, so you think that you want to wear a hat as part of your attire. My only suggestion is to not wear it religiously. There are perhaps hundreds of different types of hats worldwide with caps fitting into that category. Hats go back hundreds of years and have had its favorable periods and its not-so-favorable periods, similar to fads that come and go. America has had some very strong periods of men wearing hats to the point that it wasn't socially acceptable for a man to leave his home without wearing a hat.

I've decided to limit the number of hats down to five since I'm addressing a dress code for men. The dress hats I've chosen to talk about are the derby, fedora, top hat, panama, and cowboy hat.

Derby, American name. Bowler, English name—the bowler hat, first appeared in England in 1849, was initially made for the working class. Over time, it made its way into the middle- and upper-class people. It is a hard-felt hat made of wool, or fur felt and has a rounded crown and curled brim. The derby is considered to be a semiformal and informal attire. The bowler came to be known as the derby hat in America and was more popular in the American West than the cowboy hat, or the sombrero. Worn by lawman and outlaws, the derby gained a reputation of being the tough-guy hat. The wool felt derby can cost as little as $10 and command as much as $150 depending upon the quality of this product. The fur felt version tend to start at about $85 and can cost several hundreds of dollars.

Fedora—the fedora started out in 1882 as a women's hat. Worn in a play in America in 1889 by an actress, the fedora became a symbol of the woman's rights activists. In 1924, the prince of Wales started wearing fedoras, which started the popularity of the hat becoming a stylish hat for men. In the 1920s–1930s, the fedora became associated with gangsters, giving it the status symbol tough guy. Glorified by Hollywood's motion picture industry in the 1940s, the fedora gained in popularity into the 1950s. By the 1960s, the fedora had lost its appeal with the baby boomers as their fathers' hat. With Hollywood producing the Indiana Jones movie series with actor Harrison Ford, the fedora gained a new reputation as being the hat of the adventurer. The above leaves me with the question of "Does life imitate art, or does art imitate life"?

The fedora is a soft wide-brim dress hat with an indented crown and wide ribbon at the base of the crown, sometimes adorned with a decorative feather. Fedoras are made of straw, hemp, plastic, wool felt, cashmere, fur felt, linen, cotton, and leather. Most crushable fedoras are made of wool felt. Amazon offers the fedora for under $10 and is made of cotton or straw. Depending upon where you make your purchase will determine the quality and cost of this item. I've seen prices for linen fedoras starting at $59 and up, cotton and wool felt from $28 to $120, straw fedoras from $39 to $399, leather fedoras from $52 to $110, and fur felt from $62 to $399. As with any purchase, you have to address your need and what you're willing to spend coupled with you get what you pay for and let the buyer beware.

Top hat—made of cheesecloth, linen, flannel, and shellac, the top hat was mostly made of beaver fur and almost wiped out the North American beaver population due to supply and demand of its pelt for the mass need by the masses for top hats. Another pitfall of the top hat was the use of mercury in the production of the top hat. Mercury, being a poisonous natural material, caused many a top hat manufacturer employees to suffer from many side effects of this material to get the shine desired for the top hat. The term mad hatter came into being by a number of top hat employees going mad due to their contact with mercury on a daily basis.

Top hats were long associated as a symbol of wealth, prosperity, and the upper class and a symbol of capitalism and urban respectability due in part to the cost of owning a top hat that was equal to a month's worth of wages of the common man at the time. Top hats have fallen out of favor when in 1961, President John F. Kennedy did not wear a top hat during his presidential inauguration. President Kennedy also made the button-down collar oxford shirt popular in the workplace.

Hollywood tried to bring back the top hat by doing movie productions of Fred Astaire and Ginger Rodgers movie musical sets, just like they did with the fedora hat. However, it didn't have the same impact on the masses as the fedora did.

Since then, the top hat has only made its presence known at some high-end weddings and funerals being stately. Top hats were reduced to a status symbol of the chimney sweep, horse-drawn carriage driver, Uncle Sam posters, and the board game monopoly. Although trends, fads, and style will come and go, recently, a hip-hop performer wore a gray top hat to an awards ceremony, which could single a comeback of the top hat to its former status of wealth, prosperity, and the upper class. Only time will tell.

Panama hat—similar in design to the fedora as far as style goes. The main difference is that the panama hat is designed to keep the sunlight out of your eyes and to shield the head from the sun's rays. A product of Ecuador and the Andes, it is a woven hat made of straw from the tequila plant, a close relative of the palm.

This hat is considered to be a tropical hat due to its lightweight and breathable qualities. Although in Northern climates of both north and south of the equator, the hat has become a spring, summer, and early fall hat for a number of geographical locations depending on the current temperatures at the time.

The highest quality of panama hats have the most weave per square inch. Two thousand to four thousand weaves per square inch is not uncommon for the norm of the higher-quality product. It takes weeks to months to weave a panama hat. Just remember that, although the tighter the weave of a panama hat may represent a finer or better quality hat. I'll remind you about air circulation as opposed to hair loss due to trapped heat between the hat and the head. You can have the best of the best but at what cost?

Personally, I would prefer to buy a cheaper panama hat that has a looser weave with more ventilation as opposed to the better quality and much more expansive tighter weave of the more quality panama hats.

Pricing can range from the lowest end of a completely manufactured panama hat from $9.99 to just under $60 to a high of several hundred dollars to several thousand dollars for a completely handcrafted work of art.

Depending upon your station in life, your budget, and what you're willing to compromise on will in the determining factor to the type, cost, and the frequency that you are willing the wear such a hat. In closing all the above is a personal choice that only you can make.

Cowboy hat—ask almost any foreigner today what they think America is all about, and I'll bet you that 40 percent of them will associate America with the American Old West and the cowboy hat. This is due in part to the way that Hollywood portrayed America in movies from the 1940s through the 1960s.

The fact is that most early Americans moving West did not wear the modern Stetson cowboy hat that we associate with our wild Midwestern states as we do today. History has shown that many of the people from the East that headed West for greater opportunities, and perhaps free land, did not wear the traditional Stetson cowboy hat.

Most of the settlers at that time were wearing either bowlers (English), derbies (American), fedoras, panama hats, or sombreros.

It wasn't until between 1861–1865 that a Philadelphian haberdasher named John Batterson Stetson, who was originally from New Jersey, decided to play a joke on his friends one evening and created a hat from fur felt. Continuing to wear the hat after his joke on his friends, John Stetson ran into a rancher that offered him $5 for his hat.

This was perhaps the very beginnings of what we have become to know as the Stetson, or cowboy hat. Sometime during the promotion of the Stetson hat, it was advertised in posters as a waterproof hat depicting a cowboy giving his horse a drink of water from his hat. At some time during our history, the term ten-gallon hat had gained a reparation perhaps due to Stetson's advertisement. In fact, Stetson's hat could only hold 3.5 quarts of water.

Adding to the growth and popularity of the Stetson's style fur felt hat was the fact that the Texas Rangers and the Royal Canadian mounted police had adopted this style of hat to be a part of the regular required part of the uniform that was to be worn at the time.

In 1865, John Stetson knew that he had stumbled upon something (as with most past and modern inventions have occurred) quite by accident. In 1865, John

Batterson Stetson created his fur felt hat and started to sell his new hat, which was advertised as the boss of the plains hat, which was made to replace the sombrero and bowler. Stetson's hat had a wide brim and tall crown designed to keep the sun off the head and out of the eyes during summer months and made to keep the head warm and out of the rain during the fall and winter months. Over time, the brim was curled up so as to not interfere with the roping activities that the ranchers had to contend with when roping cattle for branding of the new calves.

Getting off subject but still on subject, I feel it's important to share with you my own personal experience during my own time frame in life. Born in 1950, at the age of fourteen, which was 1964, I was fourteen years old. The assassination of our president John F. Kennedy had just occurred. At the same time period, my brother and I were exploring the crawl space below the living room of the old farmhouse that my parents were renting for just $35 per month in Cliffwood, New Jersey, when my brother and I had discovered a civil war uniform, some leather items, and an old rusted-out gun.

Not knowing the significance of our find at the time, we gave the rusted old gun to schoolmate of our time. At fifteen years of age, I began to think in terms that from 1964 to 1864 was only a hundred-year period and how much progress we had made as a nation within such a short period of time.

In my mind, in the 1960s period, I thought that we had made a significant amount of progress within such a short period of time. Although it was the end of the industrial revolution, I hadn't known of the steam-powered locomotives turning into diesel-powered trains, nor did I know that the masses were converting from gas lighting into electric lighting, and I can go beyond.

But that would take away from the point that I'm trying to make with the fact that the Stetson Western hat was developed at the end of the civil war in 1865 and became the iconic reparation of what the American West was all about.

Some 150–160 years later, the John Batterson Stetson hat still maintains its prominence among some of the most prominent American ranchers and oil magnets of today.

Today, the well-tailored suit, a bola tie, high-quality cowboy boots, and a quality Stetson hat signifies a person of wealth and privilege, even today in 2018.

The way that one wears a hat sends a signal to the onlooker as to the message that is being delivered by the wearer of a hat as portrayed in the Hollywood movie with James Garner and Sally Fields. A man wearing a hat cocked to one side shows a cocky person, a hat worn with the brow down indicates a shy and nonconforming person, and a hat worn cocked back to expose a full face shows a person that is open, greeting new friends into his circle.

In addition to the signals of how one wears a hat, there are also social responsibilities that go along with one wearing a hat. For example, no one should ever enter into a stranger's home without taking their hat off. No one wearing a hat should ever sit down at a dinner table without taking their hat off. And no one should ever attend a church service without prior removal of their hat.

Some of our most profound and long-lasting inventions, discoveries, and hypostases have happened purely by accident by the average person's mere curiosity of what is happening in the now, or present and what can be in the future as forward thinkers.

Belts—the sole purpose of a man's belt is to hold a man's pants above the waistline of the average man. Belts can be made of leather, suede, or man-made materials that consists of a whole host of man-made synthetic materials.

Leather belts are great for the first six months that you own them, but after time with the average buckle system, they start to form a pattern on the belt holes or stations with regard to your current weight and hold and affirm that weight gain and/or loss. Meaning that the average leather belt will show signs of your comfort level to the viewer of your leather belt that perhaps you might not be so proud of.

However, the invention of the sliding and locking buckle of today can hide that fact when worn with your dress slacks, suede belts can hold the same truth as that of a leather belt. However, a leather, suede, or fabric woven belt can hold the truth about a man's fluctuating waistline.

When I was thirteen or fourteen years of age in 1963–1964, I was blessed to have come into contact with a woman named Paula Hutchinson (McGrath), who was in her sixties. Paula was a writer and illustrator of a number of children's books. Her wisdom was unselfishly shared to me in regard to the art world, but beyond that, she had shared her wisdom of what she had learned along the way on her own lifepath.

One of the most profound lessons that Paula taught me was regardless of what career path that I decided to take in life, I should apply myself to be the best in that career, and if I did so, the money would follow. I've seen this happen to others time and time again. As the saying goes, "If you love what it is that you do for a living, it's not a job, and you'll never work a day in your life. Because it's your life's passion."

Recently, I was introduced to an article by my spouse about the Japanese culture's hiring of elders to share their past experiences with the younger generations of today. To me, this is a wonderful program that can enrich the past knowledge with the future leaders of any country.

By the same token, I had a similar conversation about elders learning the pitfalls that they had experienced and trying to share, or pass onto the younger generation as to not make the same mistakes. I was rebutted by my son of twenty-somewhat years with just because a person is older doesn't make them wiser.

What my son failed to realize at the time was that not all life's lessons are written into text or are available on the Internet. It wasn't until my son was in his thirties and having gone through several of life's lessons that he began to understand the pitfalls that I was trying to share with him to avoid. Simply put, what actions that you do today can impact your future for many years to come. Although you may not recognize it at the time that you are creating your own ill-doing.

Walking sticks—the walking stick is an accessory that today we see seldom used, and if you should see one being used, it is perhaps being used by an older man. Today, walking sticks are almost always associated with old men. However, there are parts of our country or pockets where almost everyone has a walking stick. Those areas are generally mountainous areas and national parks where foot paths and trails are located for the outdoorsmen. The walking sticks can be crude branch carvings to the sophisticated city-dwelling sticks. In addition to steadying the body on unstable ground, walking sticks can also double as a defensive weapon to ward off would-be attackers. Some walking sticks are designed with a hollow tube that hides a swordlike blade that is attached to the decorative handle. I would think that in most states, they are perhaps outlawed as a lethal weapon. I would encourage you to check with your local law enforcement office with regard to the legality of such an item prior to making any purchases. You might discover that the item just isn't worth going to jail for.

Walking sticks are usually made out of hardwoods like maple, oak, and hickory, although they are also made of plastic and metal. If you feel this is a must-have accessory item that you just can't live without, do your research and find one that speaks best to serving your need and budget. In closing this segment, I'd like to add that canes are generally associated with that of elderly men that require a means beyond their own to support their bodies.

Men's canes can cost as little as $9 each to as much as $89.95 each, and today, they are offered with a tripod end support for greater stability for the user. Walking sticks, on the other hand, offer a symbol to the general public, not so much as a need to support the frame of supporting a body but more so to say that I have arrived on the financial stage, and I can afford such a luxury item as part of my attire. Walking sticks, although not used as much as they were used in the nineteenth century, still carry a certain amount of prestige to the onlookers of the general population, who might consider the cost of such an item as a frivolous expenditure, funny as it may seem. The cost of a quality walking stick will only set you back about $31 to $168.

So what you need to ask yourself is the question of is the cost and image worth the signified or powerful status symbol it represents? The rich, the middle class, and the poor all have a different perception of the symbolic message that is delivered by the opulent display of one having disposable income and how it is spent and delivered to society. Summing things up, I would say that the rich perception would be that you're on an equal, or above-equal status in society as they are and might be attracted to you as a means to bolster their own coffers. While the middle class might be inspired by your show of success and aspire their own visions to get to that rung on the ladder of success to get where you have obtained. The poor, on the other hand, seems almost always blame the rich for the fact that they haven't been able to elevate themselves out of poverty. It's always easier to blame someone else for their own shortcomings than to admit the truth that it is because of themselves that they had not succeeded in life. In short, if one were to look closely at the poorest communities in our society, one would find that most of them, if not all of them, have turned to drugs, or alcohol as a feel-good solution to their day-to-day problems. While not a fix to the issue, it is just a means to cope with their current situation, but this doesn't offer any solution to getting out of the vicious cycle of the hamster cage that they seem to be caught up in.

Wallets and money clips—every man needs a wallet. It's the place for keeping your debit and credit cards, driver's license, medical cards, and any type of identification cards that are useful to you. Wallets are also useful for carrying a spare car key, should you be so unlucky as to lock your keys in the car. Wallets can even store your money, although today, you'll find that most men don't carry money anymore thanks in part to debit and credit cards.

Perhaps the most common wallets are made of leather and are usually black, or brown in color. But your selections are endless in terms of color and materials that they are made of. Wallets don't have to be expensive. What you should focus on when buying a wallet is form and function. "Does the item fill all my needs?" and "Is the item within the price range that you're looking to spend?" should be the questions that you should be asking yourself.

Wallets can sometimes be a pain to own, especially if you're taking a long trip down the highway. A bulky wallet can become quite uncomfortable when driving for hours. A lot of truck drivers remove their wallet from their back pocket and place it somewhere in the cab of the truck prior to heading out on the road.

Money clip—in 2019, I'd take a guess that most young men don't even know what a money clip is today. I state this because from about 2001 to date 2018 technology, and we've changed on a global level with regard to the perception of the monetary ways of what we used to do in the past and what we've been accustomed to for today. Back in 1964, the president John F. Kennedy didn't carry any cash or relied upon credit or debit cards for his purchases.

Most, if not all, of you reading my book do not have knowledge of or recall the gold standard of the past. Dollar bills were produced with a red seal, which meant that you could redeem your dollars for that value in gold. A blue seal on your paper money meant that you could redeem that value in silver, and a green seal meant that you could redeem that value in paper money, or coins, which were mainly made of silver at that time.

Today, none of your paper money is backed by silver, or gold. Back in the early 1900s, Germany's money almost became worthless to the point that it took wheelbarrows of paper money just to buy a loaf of bread.

Back to my take on the money clip. To most of you, the money clip won't apply. I state this because most of you now carry a debit card linked to your bank account and/or a credit card to which you can almost make any, or all the purchases for your needs. Welcome to the new world of debits and credits, but please be aware of the pitfalls that come with other people managing your money.

Control your assets, and you control your own destiny. Give that power to someone else, and they control your destiny.

It's your choice. I carry a leather pouch money clip in my right front pocket and don't carry any money in my wallet. I find this practice to work for me. When I need cash, I know exactly where to go in the pockets of my pants. My pocket leather money clip also serves as a connivance place to store my business cards that I give out on a regular basis. I also carry a few bucks there as well for small purchases.

When the need arises to cover the cost of larger purchases, I simply reach for my debit cards that are in my wallet. If you should decide a money clip will work for your needs, then I would suggest that you find one that works best for your needs. I've found that on the low end of cost that you can expect to pay about $14.95 for a good money clip. On the high side, monogrammed with your initials could run you as much as $144. Buy what you need and serves your needs at a cost that you feel at ease with.

Lapel pins—the lapel pin is designed to be worn on the left lapel of your sports coat, or suit, just like the name implies. Fashionable among government employees and politicians but not so much among the private-sector businessman. However, some companies are now starting to award lapel pins to employees for time in service, or for extraordinary achievement and should be worn in the office as a badge of honor.

Within government, they are sometimes worn to show years of service. While politicians, congressmen, senators, and even the President of the United States wear lapel pins to show, or indicate just how patriotic they are. Most of these lapel pins are usually a United Sates flag pin.

Lapel pins with flowers are called boutonnieres and are worn at weddings, funerals, and black-tie affairs. Lapel pins cost between $7 to $14 available online, or some fine men's stores.

Umbrellas—far be it me to give you advice on umbrellas because I don't own one. In a short but true story, I'll explain why. I think the year was 1957, and at that time, I would have been seven years old. We lived in Jersey City, New Jersey. The actual apartment house address was 67 Bosewick Avenue, a side street that ran off Jackson Avenue, which is now called Martin Luther King. During the summer or early fall of that year, we had a hurricane come through named Hurricane Donna. My dad, perhaps out of drinking money, decided that he needed to send me to a store called J.J. Newberry's located about four to six blocks down on Jackson Avenue. My dad handed me a paper bag that held a pencil sharpener and give me a store receipt. He directed me to take the items and get his money back. I think the total was about $3.47. Then my dad handed me a huge black umbrella and said to me, "Now on your way and come back with the money." Like any good son, I did what I was told to do, so off I went.

Without boring you to tears, allow me to continue. I knew where the store was located because I had been to it several times prior with my mom, and it was located about the same distance in the opposite direction of my Sacred Heart Catholic Church and school that I walked to every day. So I left our downstairs apartment and headed to the enclosed vestibule toward the outside door and top porch. When I stepped out into the elements, the wind was blowing to the likes that I had never seen, or experienced before, coupled with the deluge of wind-driven rain. I proceeded to open the giant black umbrella to shield myself from the elements, and as I opened it, the wind caught the umbrella and blew the umbrella inside out. Being the quick learner that I've always been from the earliest time that I can remember, I quickly turned that umbrella and myself into the wind to undo what had just happened to me. It worked to my astonishment, and now the umbrella was back in its proper place to offer me the protection I needed from the natural elements of a hurricane. The second landing was down about six steps. I proceeded to that landing and again that umbrella blew inside out again. I applied the same process as above, and it worked again in my favor. I then made my way to the sidewalk, which, again, had the same issue. Pushing my way up the street toward Jackson Avenue, the wind just kept winning out over that umbrella. But I knew that if I was able to get to Jackson Avenue that the tides might turn in my favor. Back in the old days prior to malls most small businesses and chain stores had a preconceived standard to how storefronts and window display were to look. Most were designed of one or two panes of glass at the avenue view and carried that same glass into the overhung area of what we might call a vestibule prior to entering the store itself. This open common space allowed for a lot more window display area to showcase the many products that the store carried.

It was that open-yet-covered space that I sort on my trek to return that pencil sharpener for my dad. So when I got to Jackson Avenue, I folded up that big black umbrella and snapped it to remain closed. I felt that it had not served me well and was useless. I used those areas as a duck-

and-cover places to get out of the hurricane and to my final destination.

I made it to J.J. Newberry's drenched to the bone, sopping wet. The brown paper bag, receipt, and cardboard box that showcased the pencil sharpener were in the same tattered shape that I was. I feared that I was going to have an issue returning the item to the clerk and not be able to go back home with the money my dad expected to get. But as luck would have it, the clerk, after inspecting the item, packaging, and receipt, did refund me the money.

My trip back, I used that same storefront as shelter to get back home. Still drenched to my core, I gave my dad the refund money. It was sometime during that youth-growing period that I had decided to myself that I didn't have any need for an umbrella and carried that on into my adult life. I had, at some point, decided that it was raining that hard that I just wasn't going to out in it, and that with regular rain, we do get downpours but that they only last for short periods of time. Additionally, I thought to myself, *So it's raining. I'll dry once I get inside.* So I swore to myself I didn't need an umbrella, and to this day do not own one.

One year at work during Christmastime, we had a gift exchange. You'll never guess what I received. You guessed it. It was a collapsible compact telescoping umbrella. I stuffed it into my bottom desk drawer and left it there for years. When we moved our office to another building with modular workstations, I left that umbrella in my desk at the old building for someone who might want one.

Now just because I don't want or need an umbrella, that didn't stop me from researching the most valuable and pertinent information available to provide to you the buyer the best tools you'll need to get the best buy for your hard-earned money on buying one. Like the fedora hat, which started out as women's apparel as depicted in the 1940s movie *Casablanca*, prior to men taking it over and claiming it for themselves. The umbrella was also a woman's apparel item dating back prior to 1750. At the time, it was called a parasol and was designed to keep the sun off women and their sensitive skin. In 1750, a man grabbed a parasol and went out in public with it, which started the men's movement to claim the accessory for themselves. This was the start of what we know as the umbrella of today.

What I've learned by my research on the umbrella is the fact that once you come in from rain is that you should always leave your umbrella open to dry, prior to folding it into its compressed state. The main reason we do this is to prevent the buildup of mold on your umbrella. Folding a wet, or damp umbrella creates the perfect environment for the buildup of mold on your umbrella. So always leave your umbrella open to dry prior to storing it away.

Please visit www.artofmanliness.com for a more comprehensive knowledge on umbrellas and the many other valuable topics that this website offers to the modern man. Without going into great detail, I would suggest that the man of today stick with a basic black single or double canopy design.

Within the two basic types of umbrellas are available, the full-sized umbrella and the collapsible compact telescoping umbrella. The full-size umbrella offers a full umbrella against the elements of the weather and doubles as a defense against any street ruffians that you might encounter after hours, or late night. Some of these umbrellas are also equipped with built-in swords for your self-defense.

Today, umbrellas also come in aerodynamic designs as well as futuristic Wi-Fi designs that are capable of taking photographic pictures from your umbrella.

In closing this part of the chapter on umbrellas, I would strongly suggest that you stay away from the $5 umbrella that you'll find available on most street corners in all your major cities within the United States. You'll only get what you pay for. If you buy cheap, that is what you'll get and will last only a few seasons at best.

I've read that the very best umbrellas are made and sold in Great Britain, which stands to be, being to the fact of their average rainfall per year, they are the first and/or perhaps a close second to Seattle, Washington. So I'm tending to believe this information is true and that they do make the best. Given what I have read, it only make sense that the average cost of an umbrella in Great Britain would cost somewhere between $40 to up to $500 per umbrella.

Although I could go into the whole construction of the canopy and double canopy, frame, materials, rivets, and shaft that are the makeup of most of our current umbrellas. I won't bore you with the facts that you don't need at this time.

My personal advice would be that you pick an umbrella that fits your needs and your budget. If you're thinking that a full-sized umbrella will meet your needs of style, comfort, and protection, then I would suggest a basic black canopy of single, or double is your choice. As far as comfort, your handle should be as wide from your pinkie finger to your index finger (or pointer finger), or longer for a firm grip.

The frame should be made of nickel, brass, fiberglass, or carbon fiber to be able to withstand strong winds. Aluminum frames are cheap, light, and often don't hold up to heavy winds associated with strong wind and rainstorms. A good quality full-size umbrella might set you back on the front end by as much as $40 to $200, and in some cases as much as $500, but if you value this against a once-in-a-lifetime purchase that can last you for ten years or more, you more than likely will see the benefits over the $5 umbrella that you'll have to purchase year after year. You buy cheap, and you get cheap. "Quality never goes out of style." Everyone should know by now. We get what we pay for.

If I were to guide you as to what might be your first perfect umbrella, I would suggest a black umbrella of single, or double canopy. I would also suggest that it be collapsible, compact audio telescoping, and be automatic opening and closing. I would also suggest that you not pay any more than $20 to $55. Taken into account of the care suggestions from the manufacturer, this investment should last you for over ten years, if not longer. This in itself would bring you to a cost of about $5 per year on the high side.

Urban shoulder bag—yesterday, it was called the urban shoulder bag. A shoulder strap bag of leather, or pleather used to carry your letter-size documents to and from your office. In the 1940s, it was called a book bag, or briefcase also used to carry your letter-size documents. Not only used by office employees but also used by professors that taught in the four-year colleges. In the 1940s–50s, it was usually made of cowhide and would last your lifetime.

The 1960s–80s saw the attaché case as the most-popular device to which to carry your documents. This was a boxlike briefcase made in black, brown, or burgundy leather, had a handle and locking combination locks of brass, or silver plated.

After the fall of the attaché case by the masses came the backpack to carry your books to college and office paperwork to work. All the era changed after the 9/11 attack on the World Trade Center in New York City and the Pentagon attack in Washington, DC, when backpackers were subjected to random searches for security reasons or were prevented from entering most buildings with a backpack for the mere fact that they may contain explosives and/or a bomb.

So the urban shoulder bag came into play as the most convenient way to carry one's documents to work, or college. Easily opened for inspection, or scanned through an X-ray machine eased the time spent for building security and made it faster for the employee to go through the process of screening.

So the urban shoulder bag made its way into mainstream society for the masses. Urban shoulder bags came with a detachable shoulder strap that could be attached. Whereas the wearer could simply sling over one of his or her shoulders for the connivance of carrying. Or remove the sling to be carried as a briefcase of sorts. Although the cheaper versions of this bag were made of pleather (a fake leather), the finer quality of this item was genuinely made out of soft leather. A pleather urban shoulder bag can be purchased for about $10 to $20, and although may last you for years, most people will recognize it as exactly what it is (a cheap bag) reflecting upon your image of who you are and what you represent. Spending a few more dollars, or perhaps double the cost of the pleather urban shoulder bag will step you up into the next level of who you are and what you may represent.

Simply put, by spending $40 or upward for a soft genuine leather urban shoulder bag that will outlive you sends a message that you have arrived in the business world. It says that you know quality when you see it and are not afraid to spend the little extra money to achieve the quality you want or seek. It also says that you know that if you buy cheap, you'll get cheap. But if you buy high-quality products that the quality of the materials and craftsmanship will last your lifetime, in the long run, it will cost you far less than those that have chosen the cheaper route, who have continued to repurchase the same item over their lifetime and, in the long run, have paid twice as much as you have by buying that quality item on the front end and having it outlast your lifespan. In short, by purchasing high-quality items on the front end not only cost you less in the long run but also cost your hires less on their end.

A very simple example of this would be if you bought a soft leather document bag in the 1930s for, say, $20 at the time and used it all your life. Upon your passing, you left this bag to your elder son in, say, 1950, and he used it all his life and passed it onto his son in the 1990s who also used it for most of his life. That same $20 document bag that was passed down from generation to generation in the end would cost the last generation about $150 to obtain the same style and quality by today's standards. In closing this segment, I need to say that the rich tend to think in longer terms of their investments than that of the middle class. The middle class think in less investment terms than that of the rich as far as value of apparel items stocks, real estate, and business ventures.

While the poor seem to think in a very far different way from the middle class, or the rich. It's all about that feeling of instant gratification with them when they come into money. To show the world, or the local community, that they, at least for the moment, have the power of disposable income and purchasing power.

For the poor, it is all about the current moment and the feel-good power of having a limited power of having disposal income to the point of where they are able to buy what they want at that time, showing the local community and those around them that they are a person of means. Although this is only a temporary moment of bliss for them, because they'll have to face the moment of truth when it comes to facing the cost occurred with having to meet the cost of renting and covering the monthly utilities cost, just to keep a roof over their heads and having the basic utilities of heat, hot water, and electricity. Generally, this comes at a time when the poor will receive an income tax refund because they have fallen into the below-the-national-income standards and have fallen into the poverty levels, according to the national standards of the poor as opposed to the middle class.

Funny as it may seem, but the poor, and perhaps drug, or alcohol addicted, are the first to put their downfall blame upon the rich and middle class for their own downfall. Apparently, for the poor, it is a lot easier for them to blame others for their lack of contributing to society for their own downfall. Growing up poor myself, I have never blamed anyone for my poor beginnings but have lifted my own self up by my own bootstraps and have done all and everything needed to go from the poor to the middle-class station in life, and while I'm sixty-eight years old, I will continue to reach for getting into the realm of the rich. The poor simply just give up and only look for the happy times of drugs and alcohol to fill their misgivings of not being to be able to get to the next level of the whole class system and look for the limited happy times to fill that void.

While most of the people that grow up poor seem to reach for the stars and are willing to learn, apply, and act upon any means that will get them ahead in the world for the sake of a better lifestyle. These are the B- and C-grade students in high school who failed to give up on the American Dream of the fact that we can be anyone that we want to be going forward into the future. This means never giving up on your dreams and pushing forward to make your dreams a reality.

Chapter 10

Outerwear: Coats and Raincoats

COATS—THE COAT, BY definition, form, and function, is the most outerwear garment you'll wear. In some cases, a coat can also be called a jacket. In any case, the function is to keep you warm but can double for making a fashion statement. Generally speaking, coats are worn over shirts, sweaters, sweatshirts, suits, and jackets. The marketplace offers a wide array of coats from work, play, casual, and formal.

Coats are available in a whole host of natural materials like cotton, leather, suede, linen, wool, and hemp, just to

name a few. In addition, man-made materials—like nylon, rayon, polyester, Kevlar,
and, yes, even plastics—have made their
way into the fabric choices that designers
have looked at and used. Take that one
step further today, and you'll find that
high tech is filtering its way into the world
of garments. You might have noticed that
some materials today are being offered
as self-repair themselves from punctures.
Solar yards are being incorporated to garments to allow the wearer to charge his cell
phone and even provide heated coats.

Since my book mainly focuses on the
business attire look, I'll mainly address
only a few of these outerwear products of
the overcoat, or topcoat as it is sometimes
called. The peacoat, or three-quarter coat,
the trench coat, and the raincoat. Given
that I write about the most appealing outer
business attire. That in no way takes away
from the fact that you can achieve a great
and classy look by wearing a nice sweatshirt, blue jeans, and a bomber jacket. But

let's face it. You wouldn't want to attend a corporate business meeting, or formal affair wearing the latter.

Because I mentioned the bomber jacket or coat, I would like to talk briefly about military clothing. You might be surprised to learn that most of the outerwear that we wear today got its start by being military clothing first. The materials used and craftsmanship applied make them comfortable, durable, and easy to care for. The dress overcoat or topcoat was called the guard coat in the military. It was double-breasted and made from 100 percent wool. It was worn by soldiers that guarded posts and points of entry to sensitive areas that the military didn't want breached. Soldiers were subject to stand guard in all types of inclement weather and a downed soldier for health reasons like a cold, flu, or frostbite was of little use to the military in protecting its compound. Other coats that started as military clothing prior to becoming civilian clothing were the trench coat (Army), peacoat (Navy), and parka used in the Arctic and Antarctic.

Overcoat/topcoat—the overcoat or topcoat as it is sometimes called is a must for the well-dressed man. It is your fall and winter dress coat worn over your business suit. Overcoats are mainly made from 100 percent wool and fall below the knee and above the calf. Overcoats are available in a wide range of colors and patterns, but your best bet would be to buy one that isn't going to out of style within a few years because of some current fad. For economic reasons, a quality overcoat can cost you $300 to $500 and in some cases even more. For that reason, you'll want to get the biggest bang for your buck. If you stick to the basics I'm about to outline for you, this will be a once-in-a-lifetime purchase. Best bets are the beige wool, or cashmere overcoat if the majority of your dress wardrobe of suits are in the brown tones. The gray (light or dark), navy blue, and black are perhaps the most-favored colors.

Topcoats are available in hidden buttons, single button, and the double-breasted. Depending upon your age, you should take into consideration your growth and weight patterns. If you think that you may have stopped growing and have reached your normal natural weight, then I'd suggest that you buy your overcoat that has a slightly tailored look to it. If you tend to gain or lose ten to twenty pounds of weight over a season, then you might want to stay away from that tailored look because nothing looks tackier than wearing a topcoat that looks like it's too small for you because the fabric is pulling on the buttons. Please note that when you go to buy your overcoat, you need to be wearing a business suit since this coat is made to be worn over that suit. If you take my advice in this area, you'll get the best fit and look.

Best places to buy an overcoat for less would be the Internet; however, the drawbacks are that you won't be able to try the garment on, and sometimes, the color photo of the item might be deceiving.

Since most men buy the basic colors, the overcoat doesn't go out of style, like some of the other clothing. So vintage clothing will yield you the greatest savings, and thrift stores are your best bet. When searching out a thrift store, look for one that would be located in the wealthiest neighborhoods near you.

Peacoat—the peacoat, as it was called in the military and sometimes called in civilian life, is also known as the three-quarter coat and, at times, called a car coat. The peacoat, like the overcoat, are mostly made of heavy wool with broad lapels and are hidden button, single-breasted, and double-breasted. Never buy a zippered peacoat because the association is with that of a child's coat. The most common colors are gray (light and dark), black, and navy, or dark blue. The cost range is less than $100 to over $100. Compared to the average cost of an overcoat costing $300.

This makes this coat the perfect alternative to buying an overcoat. The three-quarter length of this coat means that you can wear it over a suit, and the bottom of the suit jacket will not extend beyond the length of the peacoat, which would look tacky and very unprofessional.

Wool care—since I just covered two wool coats, I deem it time to point out the proper care of these garments. You now realize that a wool coat isn't a cheap piece of apparel, and when we get to the chapter of student and men's suits, you'll probably be purchasing a heavy and light-weight wool suit as well. One of the main drawbacks to owning wool clothing, be it a sweater, suit, or outercoat, is the moth. Moths can convert a fine garment and turn it into rag material before you know what has happened. There are several ways to propel these pesky little pests.

What comes to mind first is the now-outdated hope chest, which was stored at the foot of the bed. The hope chest, for those of you that aren't familiar with, was a storage box sometimes locking that women stored their most valuable fabrics of bedding and clothing. Cedar is a natural moth repellent, and some of the hope chest were made completely of cedar. The less-expensive models of the furniture were just cedar lined. Next came the cedar-lined closets, which offered the same protection from moths and other insects. Today, they might have available cedar-lined armoires. Your clothing will remit the slight scent of the cedar oils. Another possible alternative is the use of cedar chips or shavings. The plastic zippered garment bag may also work for you to solve this problem.

The next cheaper method is the use of what is called moth balls readily available at most grocery, box stores, and hardware stores. Using mothballs will leave a greater unpleasant scent on your garments. My last suggestion to save your fine wool items is the use of a product called diatomaceous earth powder, or boric acid powder. If you've already come under attack by moths, you'll need to sprinkle this product on your existing wool products to kill any remaining moth eggs or larvae. After applying this powder, you'll also have to vacuum your clothing and the area that your clothing was stored in to remove any eggs or larvae that might still remain. Once the storage area is cleaned, you'll need to dust the area with the diatomaceous earth powder, or boric acid powder. When this process is done, you can restore your wool garments. One last note: always dry clean any of your wool garments as stated on your care label.

Trench coat—the trench coat dates back over a hundred years and has a military association. Trench coats are made of semiwaterproof fabric or completely waterproof materials and are designed to shed water. Trench coats are also made of leather. This long knee-to-calf-length outerwear garment has an industry standard of including a belt, button-down shoulder straps called epaulets, and cuff straps made from the same material as the rest of the garment. During my time in the military, the trench coat shoulder straps were used to store the soldier's garrison cap and/or his black leather dress gloves. The cuff straps were used to prevent rain from trickling down the arms. The upper vents located below each shoulder on the front and back of this garment were incorporated in the military trench coat to expel body order from the soldier that was out in the field perhaps too long. The trench is made with deep front pockets that were originally designed for the soldier to be able to carry his maps.

This garment was made in single and double-breasted. Available colors today are beige, browns, ivory, white, grays, black, greens, and navy blue. This garment can serve as a raincoat for snow, light rain, and wind. This garment can be used in place of the overcoat over your suit but doesn't offer the warmth that the overcoat does. Cost-wise, a trench coat will, in most cases, cost you a lot less than an overcoat and can serve as a cheaper alternative to the overcoat. My best source suggestion for saving you the consumer money would be eBay as long as you know your clothing size or measurements. eBay offers new, new without tags, vintage, and used. The biggest drawback is that you can't try on the item prior to the purchase, but I've found the pricing, to me, is great.

Because the trench coat has been worn by some disrupting groups of young people, some school districts have added this garment to their dress code policy as an item of clothing that is not allowed to be worn on school grounds. Our clothing, regardless of the piece, can sometimes come with a positive or negative association to that piece. With that said, I'll mention zoot suits, beatniks, and Nehru jackets.

Raincoats—the raincoat truly does date back hundreds of years, at least some form of raincoat does. Man has been devising ways and means of keeping the rain off him for decades, if not centuries. Natural materials used include animal skins and hides to include animal furs, animal guts, plant leaves, straws, and fibers.

The most noted inventor of a waterproof fabric for tarpaulin, which became widely used in the making raingear, is Charles Macintosh, a chemist from Scotland, who, in 1823, used natural rubber dissolved in naphtha and coated two pieces of cloth to sandwich a waterproof material. Today, this process is known as vulcanization.

About the 1950s, the development of polyvinyl chloride (PVC) in sheet form. This product became known as vinyl. This material became very popular during the 1960s and seventies as the in-fashion material used in all types of clothing. Raingear, like raincoats and umbrellas, swept the marketplace. This material used in rain-coats was excellent at repelling rainwater. One of the drawbacks of this material used in raincoats was that it became stiff if worn in cold weather. The other draw-back was that this material doesn't breathe. Having material that is able to breathe is very important because it allows our body heat a method of escape.

While vinyl clothing is still made and worn today, it has been given an associa-tion to fetish clothing, which as I've stated before that some garments have gained a reputation connected to them that can produce either a positive or negative image depending on the current values of society at that time.

The next period of waterproof mate-rials that changed raingear came with the invention of a product called Gore-Tex. This material was lightweight and offered good breathability. Gore-Tex by itself is not a suitable material for the making of raingear and so it has to be vulcanized with other layers of fabrics. Without doubt, man will keep looking for new ways to improve upon the materials and fabrics used in the manufacture of raingear to keep us comfortable and the elements of the weather off our backs.

London Fog, perhaps one of the most recognized brand names for high-quality and style raincoats, was founded as the Londontown clothing company in Baltimore, Maryland, in 1923. At sixteen years of age, Israel Myers went to work for the company. In 1930, the company failed, and in 1931, Mr. Myers purchased the name and physical assets of the company that was making tailored men's clothing and topcoats. During World War II, the company made waterproof clothing for the United States Navy. After the war, the company partnered with the DuPont Company to make material for use in the making of raincoats. These raincoats were the first to offer the zip-out coat liner, which made this garment a year-round garment. During the 1960s and '70s, two-thirds of all raincoats sold in America were London Fog—further proof that quality and craftsmanship never go out of style. London Fog's first civilian raincoat was introduced in 1954 as a trench-coat-style raincoat. Today, the company is owned by Iconix Brand Group, Herman Kay Company Inc., and offers a full line of clothing and accessories.

Those of you young men who are struggling to build your wardrobes, if you don't think at this time that you can afford to buy new, I'd suggest that you seek out a vintage London Fog raincoat from the Internet or secondhand outlets to meet your current needs. Later, you can buy new, and you pass on your vintage prize to one of your siblings. Again, I'll state, "Quality never goes out of style."

Chapter 11

Jackets, Suits, and Seasonal Periods

JACKETS—IN MY MIND, jackets should be broken up into two distinguished and separate groups. The first group pertains to casual attire and the everyday outer clothing that is worn daily in the blue-collar industries. It is the outerwear that is worn after work, if one were to work in an office environment. This casual outer clothing associated with the outdoorsman on camping, fishing, hiking, and exploring venues. It's the type of clothing that one would wear to the baseball, football, hockey games, or just trekking around the neighborhood, or visiting the local lumberyard.

When I think of this type of jacket, I think in terms of wearing it with T-shirts, sweatshirts, sport shirts, Henleys, and, yes, even dress shirts. I also think in terms of wearing it with jeans, khakis, corduroy, and some dress slacks. All depends upon the type of activity you'll be engaging in.

These jackets are available in an array of designs, colors, and materials that encompass both natural and man-made. By basic standards, these jackets are usually midstomach in length with zippered, or buttoned fronts. They come in a host of different weights depending upon the jacket being worn in the spring/summer, or fall/winter. Naming just a few of the most popular styles that have stood the test of time and still, to this day, remain fashionable. They are the flight jacket, bomber jacket, windbreaker, rain jacket, denim jacket, and the varsity/baseball jacket.

The frugal buyer will be able to fill his wardrobe needs of these jackets if he has prepared himself to knowing exactly the type of jacket he is interested in procuring and has done his homework. This applies to buying new, used, or vintage. Understand what it is that you want, what a fair price is, what is the quality and craftsmanship, and what the reputation of the brand is. Follow these simple steps, and you'll get the best product at the lowest possible price.

Jackets: Suit Jackets

My second group of jackets pertain to the well-dressed casual look of the jacket, and in this term, I think of the suit jacket and only the jacket that may or may not have been part of a suit. Although this jacket also represents the casual look, it is representative of an upscale version and speaks business relaxed. Many old worn-out suits still have an excellent jacket that is salvageable. In fact, the slacks are the first piece of a suit to wear out. For that very reason, finer suits will come with two pairs of slacks to get a longer life out of that expensive suit.

The suit jacket worn with a nice dress shirt (no tie), open collar, and a pair of nice jeans (no soils), or pressed khakis with a nice pair of shoes will speak volumes to any onlooker as to who you are and where you come from. The corduroy jacket (with, or without the leather, or suede elbow patches) makes a fine presentation. The same applies to the tweed, canvas, and linen jackets for that casual but special look.

Jackets: The Versatile Navy-Blue Blazer

This is yet another piece of clothing that started out as a military uniform that made its way into business-world attire. If my research is correct, this jacket was once a British officer's uniform. Later, this blazer, which started out being called a reefer jacket, was worn by Ivy League colleagues rowing teams to keep them warm during cold training exercises.

This jacket, made from flannel, or wool and loosely fitted in the beginning before getting its tailored look, is available in a host of colors, but my focus is on the dark blue, or black blazer in single or double-breasted. Although available in a number of button styles, stick with the brass buttons for the best look. An embodied emblem patch on the top front pocket indicating what college, or university you were from. My blazer has a Ralph Lauren (polo) patch on the pocket. If you purchase a blue blazer that doesn't come with a pocket patch, you can personalize your blazer by searching out an embodied family crest or coat-of-arms patch and having your local tailor or dry cleaners sew on for a few dollars. Research has shown that there over a dozen companies making embroidered family patches on the Internet. Some have minimum orders, while others do not. Iron-on versions are available by some companies. The average cost is about $25 to $40 for a single patch. Prices go down on volume orders.

Young men who are just starting out to build their business-attire wardrobe collection, I highly recommend that you seek out and purchase one of these blazers as your first jacket. In the fashion and clothing industry, we rarely find a garment that can last the test of time. Fads and current trends generally only last for a few years, or maybe a decade. But true classics will carry themselves for many decades. In time, you'll find that your blazer becomes one of your most-favored jackets because of its wide range of possible looks that you can achieve.

Clothing, like many other things in our lives, has an association, or reputation affiliated with it. The blazer is associated with officers of the military and schools of higher learning. Onlookers assume that you're smart, knowledgeable, or intelligent by first impressions alone.

I called it the versatile blazer for a reason. It's considered upscale casual. This one jacket can be worn with a same-color pair of slacks, and now, you look like you own a suit. Wear it with gray, beige, ivory, or white slacks, and you project another image of yourself. Wear it with khakis, or blue jeans, and you've achieved yet another entirely different look. Put on a contrasting color, silver, or gold vest under your blazer, and you've created your own fashion statement.

For additional stylish looks, it can be worn with a turtleneck, oxford dress shirt with, or without a dress tie, add a V-neck thin sweater, and again, another image emerges. The possibilities are endless and only limited by your imagination and your full-length mirror. I state the mirror because some of your combinations just might not work. The colors that you choose and style of shirt you pick must compliment the blazer and not clash with it, so just be mindful and don't be afraid to ask your mom, or sister how you look.

The cost factor—today, while researching my subject matter, I took notice to a Brooks Brothers's navy-blue blazer with brass buttons in a computer advertisement. Brooks Brothers was offering their beautiful high-quality blazer for $648. Since my book is geared toward boys and young men that are between the ages of fourteen to thirty, I don't expect that you'll have the disposable income resources to go out and buy the top of the line. I also came across a Hickey Freeman wool navy-blue blazer for $995, while J. C. Penny offered a blazer for $39.99. It all boils down to we get what we pay for. Additionally, my message is to awaken your senses in terms of saving you money while teaching you about quality at the same time. For my young readers out there, pick a price range to what you can afford while inspecting and comparing it to quality, or lack of quality that is built into your purchase. It's always better in the long run to pay a little more to get the quality that you want. The cheapest is not always the best buy.

Jackets: Double-Breasted Jacket or Suit

Long associated with the look of a banker, and perhaps nothing speaks more about money than having the look of a banker. The beginning for the double-breasted jacket wasn't met well in the business world. It was considered to be too casual attire to be worn in the office environment and rejected by most businesses. Of course, I'm speaking of a time prior to the 1930s. In the 1930s–40s, the double-breasted suit made its way to become proper formal wear. Today, this jacket and/or suit is a staple among menswear and fashion and has grown to represent an image of power and money.

Suits—man's very basic survival depends upon a few must-have needs: food (because with no food in three weeks, man will die), air (because without air, one will die within a minute), water (within three days without water, man will die), shelter, and clothing from the elements of earth. I mention this because we talk about the subject of men's suits, which are outer garments designed to protect the body from the elements but more so today to present an extended, or external vision of who we are and what we are about. Clothing represents an almost-neon sign of advertising of the person beyond the clothes, and as I've stated earlier, our clothing is an extension of ourselves in the same way that our automobiles are but on a grander scale. They, too, are also extensions of who we are, based upon what we drive. For that very reason is why Americans have fallen so much in love with the automobile, which they realized was a further extension of who they were on another layer of presentation to the public. The same holds true for the type of house or home that we live in. It, too, suggests to the public the status in life that we have achieved.

Today, there are perhaps more makers and manufacturers of children, student, and men's suits than neither you nor I could even count. For ease of understanding, I've decided to do a flowchart on the subject of men's suits. Starting with the worst, or cheapest to the finest in men's suits.

Suits: Worst and Cheapest

Perhaps the worst, or cheapest suit that one could buy would be a suit jacket that has no liner built into the suit jacket. This suit would normally have only two buttons on the sleeve and only two buttons on the front of the jacket.

The industry standard is that the more buttons sewn onto the outer sleeves of the jacket is the indicator or barometer to

judging the suit's quality and craftsmanship of the garment. The amount of inside
pockets and coin or watch pockets that the
suit jacket has also provided another clue
as to the quality of the suit. Always keep
in mind the amount of amenities that are
built into a suit. If you pay attention to
the subtle amenities that one suit has over
another, you will always be buying the better suit. The slacks associated with this suit
also have some telltale signs in terms of the
quality of the suit. For example.

If the suit slacks don't offer any back
pockets, or only one back pocket to the
slacks, it means that the maker, or manufacturer is looking for ways to cut costs
in the making of the garment. Also, if a
coin, or as in the old days, a watch pocket
isn't provided, it is a further indication of
a lesser-quality-made suit. Having given
you all the basic parameters of what makes
a quality suit over a nonquality suit, I'd
like to finish up with the fabric that the
suit is made up of. A cheat suit of this

group will be made from a cotton fabric. While a finer-made garment of this design will more than likely be made of linen. In closing this segment on worst, or cheapest suits, I would simply like to state that an unlined fine-linen-made suit with all the bells and whistles of inside jacket pockets and slack pockets would be the best quality and craftsmanship of the perfect type of suit that one would want to purchase for the summer, or for any tropical location that one might be stationed in. Let the craftsmanship and quality guide you whether you are buying new, or used.

Suits: Better Buy

Perhaps the next best-quality and craftsmanship suits are that you can purchase would be the three-button-sleeve suit. This is the first indication of a better-made suit. I state this because every little addition that is added to the making of a suit adds an additional cost to the manu-

facture of that suit. Thus, it raises the man-
ufacturing and retail cost of that suit to the
public. Simply stated, the consumer pays
for everything. Just because the designer
or manufacturer has decided to add a button to the sleeve of their jackets of their
suits doesn't necessarily mean that you
are buying the best or even better-quality suit. Typically, these suits were made
with half or fully lined. One must check
all the added amenities that are offered to
that three-button suit as outlined above to
decide if your purchase warrants paying a
higher price for what you may think is a
better-quality men's suit. As noted above,
please take into consideration the amount
of extra inside jacket pockets and slack
pockets are being offered with this suit
whether buying used from a thrift shop or
new from the retailer.

At this point, I've decided to go a little
off subject on my flowchart suits to further educate my readers. I'm going to be
brazing enough to assume that most, if not

all, of my current readers were born after 1960. Given that I've made that statement, I will simply state that, as the author, I was born in 1950. But based upon my research in writing my book, I have done an enormous amount of research prior to what I have written. During that research, I've discovered that during the period of 1941–1945, the World War II period, that not only was our own military stretched to its limit on personal sacrifice but that the whole nation of the United States of America also paid the price of national rationing—no longer could men's suits of the 1940s and their very wide lapels and cuffed and pleated pants sustain the war effort. During the Great War, civilian men were forbidden to buy suits with any lapels, cuffs on suit slacks were also forbidden, and the slacks could not exceed nineteen inches in width on the legs. These measures were put into effect because the nation felt that they needed these extra materials to make uniforms for our troops that were fighting the war.

With change sometimes comes a new revolutionary change. Born after the Great War, a baby boomer, as my generation has been labeled, came the invention of the continental look in men's suits of owning a suit that had no cuffs on its slacks. Polyesters were a new material at the time, and what was called shark skin were introduced as the new in fabric of the time. Manufacturers at the time rejoiced at the acceptance by the masses of the baby boomers because it meant a lower cost of production and higher retail cost to the consumer, producing greater profits for the manufacturer. In closing this segment, I'll simply state as I have before. As time goes on, "*we pay more and get less.*"

Suits: Best Buy

Perhaps the most-recognizable feature of a best suit would be indicated by the amount of buttons sewn on to jacket sleeves. Four buttons is an industry standard today. Men tend to take notice of these small but significant details, whereas, most woman fail to take notice. Your best-buy suit jacket should be fully lined and possesses at least two inside pockets and perhaps a change pocket. While your slacks to this suit should have two rear pants pockets and even a change pocket by itself or sewn into the right front pocket of your slacks.

Before I write about the very best and perhaps most extreme and expensive clothing in men's suits and clothing in the current fashions of the times that are available today on the market with regard to quality and craftsmanship, I'd like to take a moment to discuss that as time passes on, we'll pay more and get less with regard to the quality and craftsmanship that our forefathers paid and enjoyed.

As a simple example of this, I would like to reference the cost and quality of the average topcoat of the 1930s. The average cost of a supreme quality topcoat of the time was between $29 and $34 for the finest hand-sewn best material available on the market garment. This same principle was applied to men's suits and other apparel. As stated above, the same quality and craftsmanship built into a quality men's overcoat, or suit would cost you anywhere from the low end of $300–$500 to the high end of $800–$5,000 depending upon the designer and brand of the garment.

Hence, as I've said all along, "As time goes by, we can expect to pay more and get less" in terms of any, or all the consumer products that we purchase. In short, it's called economic inflation; whereas, the manufacturers are looking for ways to cut the cost of the goods that they are producing to maintain their profit margin to be able to still remain in business. In a balancing act, have the consumer not feel

CARL H. BECKER III

that they are paying more than a garment is worth.

Shorting the paraphrase of this, I'll simply state that when the economy is good, clothing manufacturers will give you less materials at a higher cost. While in a bad economy, these same clothing manufacturers will offer you wider dress ties and double-breasted suits at the same pricing as the narrower dress ties and single-button men's suits just to attract business in lean times to be able to stay afloat.

Prior to my writing about the extreme best quality of young teens and men's suits, I feel compelled to educate you on the ways of the middle class, or poor as I grew up. I state this for your decade to perhaps gain a greater understanding of what your generation has taken for granted, and what your generation seems to think is your right. As I've stated in the past, as we go forward in life, we will pay more and get less. To the person that has reached a six-figure salary from their job, this information may seem meaningless. But to the average man, this information is of great value.

Growing up in a poor environment meant to me that I paid particular attention to the fact that my dad was an alcoholic and that my mother suffered from his lack of as my dad to be the proper provider of the family needs, which caused my mother to suffer nervous breakdowns to the point that I and my two siblings were forced to fend for ourselves.

Funny, as it might seem, but the early struggles of our lives prepared all of us for what we might face in the future. My brother, sister, and myself have run into situations with coworkers that have complained about the simplest obstacles in life that we looked upon as child's play from the background that we had come from. Life is certainly funny when we view it from the past, present, and future.

I state all the above for a very serious reason. Growing up, we learned that a few basic goods were needed for us to sustain life and living. We would purchase at the beginning of a month a 50-pound bag of potatoes, 10 pounds of flour, 5 pounds of sugar, and a few other staples. At the time, a 50-pound bag of potatoes cost only $2.50 and would last the month. Pasta was also a cheap item to buy that would sustain us through the month. Further evidence observed that support my saying of "as time goes on, we will pay more and get less" comes with the fact that in the 1960s, sugar distributors started repackaging the 5-pound bag of sugar into 2 1/2-pound bags. I knew at the time that the 2 1/2-pound bag was going to cost the consumer the same amount of money as the cost of the 5-pound bag of sugar. It was all a matter of time, and I was right on my assumption. My point being is that these very humble beginnings taught myself, my brother, and my sister to be conservative of what we had and how to stretch a dollar for what we truly wanted in life. Teaching us the value of quality into our purchasing power. In the end, it doesn't matter where you came from in the station of life that you were born into. It's all about the journey and where you wind up in the end.

Suits: Extreme Best Suit Buys

Perhaps I've fallen a little behind on the best of the best-quality in men's suits. Growing up, I understood that the finest of men's suits came with two pairs of slacks. Although, recently, I discovered that two pairs of matching suit slacks are no longer available.

Just another cost savings associated with the manufacture being able to make a profit on the production of its goods that it presents to the marketplace. Caveat emptor—let the buyer beware.

I'm almost sure that if one were willing to pay for a custom-made suit and insisted that it came with two pairs of matching slacks that you would be able to find a tailor to accommodate your needs.

In your case, it's more than likely that even your best suit will come off a rack of premade suits that may or may not include some tailoring depending upon the retailer that you choose. Your best-made suits will include more inside and outside pockets than you'll ever need. In fact, some of the pockets will come with pockets within the pockets. For example, your suit jacket may have a change pocket sewn into your inside, or outside pocket.

The same holds true for your pants pockets. I noticed that on some of my suits that the change pocket is almost always built into the right front pocket of the slacks. This indicates to me that most right-handed men keep their billfold in that pocket and their keys in the left pocket of the slacks as I do. Pocket flaps and buttoned pocket flaps on the inside of your suit jacket, or rear pockets of your suit slacks is another telltale sign of a quality suit. The term deep pockets, as most of you are probably not unaware of, tends to mean that the person having deep pockets is a person of means and has disposal income money to spend.

I have an issue about a pants's front pocket depth for several reasons. My first objection comes from the fact of a suit made with small-depth pockets indicates to me that the clothing manufacturer is looking for a way to cut cost of materials in order to gain an edge on his competitors of being able to offer a suit for less than them. My second issue with smaller-than-normal, or expected pants pockets is the fact that when in the sitting position, some of your pocket items can and will drift out of your pocket and land on the chair, or couch you have rested upon without your notice, causing you to lose keys, pocket knives, lighters, and money. Another issue that I have with appeal makers is the sizing of the rear left wallet pocket on the slacks. Believe me when I say that no man wants to struggle getting his wallet out of this pocket for presentation to deliver a debit, or credit card at the time of a purchase—most embarrassing at the time.

The amount of buttons on the jacket sleeve and whether they unbutton or not is another measure of a quality suit. In short, the more that is built into a suit in terms of time needed to sow the suit together with the materials (fabrics) used and the amount of buttons used (four on the jacket sleeve) all come into play to terms of the quality and price you'll pay for the finest garment. You'll also find that the better-made suits will almost always come with the outside jacket pockets sewn closed. I think that the manufacturer does this practice for the purpose of creating the best look of the suit jacket. I like to be able to use all the available amenities that are built into the suit that I am buying. Hence, I will grab a seam ripper and remove the stitching from the outside jacket pockets as well as the inside jacket pockets to make them all available for my needs. By the same content, I'll state that my latest boss would never remove the stitched pockets on any of his newest suits. When I confronted him on this subject, he stated that "by keeping them stitched, it insured that clean tailored look of the suit" as the manufacturer intended it to look. Whereas, I differed from my boss's point of view on the stitching of the pockets. Upon my purchasing of a new suit, if I found that the pockets were stitched, I would grab a seam ripper and carefully remove all that stitching to make them operable and useable. Being concerned by the outward appearance, I would never place any object into these pockets that was going to appear outwardly bulky giving that sloppy appearance. But if needed, I had the pockets available for their intended purpose.

Dress shirts—I bring up the subject of the men's dress shirts at this time because it is almost directly related to the man's suits. It was President John F. Kennedy that made it possible for the average business-man to be able to wear a button-down-collar oxford to the workplace because he had set the president. The same applies to the Duke of Windsor who made it possible for the double-breasted suit jacket and suit as well as some other brazing contributions that he contributed to men's fashions that still remain to this day.

I bring up all the above information for a reason. That reason is to point out to you, my reader, that back in 2005, I took notice of the fact that a number of men in the workplace started to wear their dress shirts untucked from their slacks, or pants creating a casual business look. It presented itself as a clean casual look, which made them stand out from their peers. In 2018, or before, I noticed Internet companies advertising that style by cutting back on the tail as it is called on a man's shirt as a cleaner look than the regular dress shirt with the longer tail.

Whereas, I agree with their concept to a certain point as far as the look is concerned. I disagree to the point that they are looking to charge the consumer $85 for one of their shirts. First of all, it will require the company to spend about 25 percent less on the fabric materials than their competitors. Secondly, you've now purchased a shirt that can be worn only one way, which is outside your trousers. Ask any man what is the worst or most-annoying issue when dressed up, and I can grant you that it is the fact of the dress shirt rising out of their trouser because the tail of the shirt is too short that they will have to constantly have to make the time to tuck it back into the slacks. So ask yourself, is the increased cost of this new in look and the limited use of this garment worth the price?

Mixing and Matching: To Create Your Own Individual Fashion Style

Today, it almost seems to be common-place that each decade is searching for or looking to create their own personal style. The younger generations are in constant turmoil to not dress as their fathers and grandfathers did and are seeking their own identity, style, and fashion to be identified with as a generation. Trends and fads had their heyday. Vintage clothing also had its day. But with each and every genera-tion, it seems to become more difficult for them to achieve their own brand-ing identification. Here is a bit of trivia pertaining to clothing. A recent survey stated that we Americans will spend about $1,700 a year on new clothing and that on average, Americans either throw out or donate about 65 pounds of clothing per year. Today, some thrift stores are receiv-ing so much volume of used clothing that they are starting to reject the older vintage clothing and seek to take in only more-current clothing. This mere fact signifies that the conscious young man on a budget can build his starting wardrobe for pennies on the dollar.

Perhaps the newest or latest trend might become that of mixing the tried-and-true traditional, classic look with that of the uniforms of the working-class trades to create an entirely new look that would be accepted in the fashion world of a new style. Maybe, and just maybe, 1 to 2 percent of these new looks may become classics on their own, holding up to the timeless look for generations to come.

Being the forward thinker that I sometimes think that I am, I'm willing to say that "the turtle doesn't get anywhere, unless he sticks his neck out." I offer the suggestive advice of mixing the work-recognized uniform of the doctor and his lab coat; the farmers' overalls, or as it's called in the mining industry, bibs; the chief's shirt, or jacket; the bowling shirt as promoted in the TV series of *Two and a Half Men* as worn by the actor Charlie Sheen; the workmen's uniform of matching shirt and pants; the horse jockey uniform; and the clothing worn by the car and motorcycle racing world, like Indy and motocross drivers. Here is a style that you might want to entertain. Maybe this style will bring back the man look in men. Try mixing a plaid flannel shirt with solid-color slacks and a solid-color sports jacket. I've experimented with this concept and found that while the flannel shirt speaks to the ruggedness of the man, the other garments speak to refinement, giving the look that says, "I'm rugged and refined." By your own imagination, there is no telling what you may come up with as your own personal style that might catch on to the mainstream American fashion style and become a new classic within the fashion industry adopted by the masses.

Chapter 12

Clothing Care and Dry Cleaning

READ THE CLOTHING care label. I can't stress this information enough, so I'll state it again. Read the clothing care label. In 1961, or 1962, when I was eleven or twelve years old, I started to do my own laundry at the laundromat. I didn't read the garment care labels on any of my clothing but just tossed, or sometimes stuffed my clothes into the washing machine. I'd set the washer on hot water, thinking it was the best setting for getting my clothes really clean, and I'd add the laundry detergent, and sometimes I would even add bleach.

One day while doing my laundry, I tossed in a sweater of mine, and after the wash and the dryer, I proceeded to the folding part of the job. When I got to my sweater, it had shrunk to a size that only a four-year-old child could wear.

During this same period of time, I started experimenting with clothing dyes. Although there were signs hanging up in the laundromat stating "*no dying of clothes*," I simply choose to just ignore them. Each week, I would add my dye packet to my wash load, and in the end, I would wind up with all-pink shirts. The next week, they would all come out of the washer as all-blue shirts. The last that I remember was that all my clothes came out looking gray. I'm sure that the women at that laundromat just loved me.

If the care label states to wash in warm water, follow the instructions and do as it instructs. The same holds true with any garment stating *dry clean only*. If, for some reason, you don't want to spend the money by bringing your dry clean items to the dry cleaners, you do have an alternative, which is sold at your local grocery store. The item that I'm talking about is a home dry clean kit. Two of these kits are the *Dryel* brand and the *Woolite* brand. The *Dryel* kit costs around $11 plus sales tax and is good for four-home dry cleaning cycles. Each cycle will dry clean four garments at a time, which means that for the whole kit, you'll get sixteen items dry cleaned at home for a cost of around seventy-five cents per garment. Compare that cost to having your local dry cleaner doing it for you, and you can expect to pay about $7 per item or more for such items like sweaters, suits, and jackets. So you can see that the at-home dry cleaning self-service will save you money, but it does cost you in time, and we all know that time is money. The kit contains a plastic bag with air holes in it and a dry clean packet that you add to the bag with your garment. Read the directions and place the bag with your garment, or garments into your cloth dryer.

Another alternative to dry cleaning establishments and the at-home dry cleaning systems for some of your wool garments would be to wet wash with a product like Woolite. I caution you to not wet wash a wool suit. Dry cleaners will do a much better job, so why risk destroying your garment? My advice is geared toward wet washing your other wool clothing, like sweaters and shirts. I offer a few warnings relating to wet washing any wool garment: (1) never use bleach it will dissolve the wool fibers; (2) never wash in hot water; (3) never use a clothes dryer because it will cause your garment to shrink; (4) never dry your garment in direct sunlight because it can cause your garment to fade from the rays of the sun; and (5) never hang your wet garment when looking to dry it. The weight of the water contained in your garment will cause your garment to stretch out of shape. After rinsing, lay your clothing item on a clean dry towel and roll your garment in the towel to remove excess moisture from clothing. With another clean dry towel, lay flat on a solid surface, like a table, to dry. Should you decide to try this method, read the directions on the jar and follow the manufacturer's directions.

Almost every small town has a dry cleaner, and some small towns and cities have multiple dry-cleaning establishments. The small towns and cities that have many dry cleaners offers you the opportunity to shop and price compare to get you the lowest price. I did that when it came to having my dress shirts cleaned and extra heavy starch pressed. Because I drop off my shirts in volume—meaning eighteen, twenty-five, thirty at a time—grants me to be in a bargaining and negotiating position. I have reduced the cost per shirt by twenty-five cents per shirt playing the competition game. With that said, I'll remind you of my old quote of "*After birth, death is inevitable. Everything else is negotiable.*"

I've also had some bad experiences with dry cleaners. One that comes to my mind are the shirts that kept coming back with broken buttons. It seems that the presser at the cleaners was slamming down the press onto the shirts and breaking the buttons. I changed dry cleaners to solve that problem.

Today, we also have national chains of dry cleaners that operate across the country. Since these national chains of dry cleaners already offer the lowest prices available in the marketplace, I don't think that you'll stand a chance in trying to get a lower price based on volume. Dry cleaning is a nine-billion-dollar industry.

Martinizing Dry Cleaners—founded in 1949, or as I remember them as One Hour Martinizing—had as many as 580 locations in 2007 but today has only 379 locations.

Comet Cleaners founded in 1957 had 261 locations in 2010 and currently has 175 locations.

Tide Dry Cleaners in 2009 had sixty locations that offers a GreenEarth eco-friendly cleaning system, which I think means the same as Elite Cleaners, which uses hydrocarbon solvents over the per-chloroethylene solvents, which is safer for our environment.

Zips Dry Cleaners, founded in 1996, is a Greenbelt-based cleaner that operates in the Washington, DC, Maryland, Virginia, and as far west as Pittsburgh, Pennsylvania. In 2015, they had thirty-nine stores with a five-year goal to have over 350 stores across the country. They tout the any-garment dry cleaned for $1.99.

Dryclean Depot, a Houston-Texas-based firm, has moved into the market-place of Zips, DC, market offering $1.75 for any garment and 99¢ for any shirt.

Dryclean, USA, in 2007, had 473 locations in the United States and 305 locations overseas.

OXXO Care Cleaners had twenty locations in 2007. Today, they have over fifty locations. OXXO uses the GreenEarth cleaning equipment and solvents.

One more closing word about dry cleaners. In addition to being able to have your dry clean items done and your dress shirts washed, starched, and pressed, today, most dry cleaners offer expert clothing alteration services to give your garments that custom-tailored look. In addition to the alteration service, many dry cleaners today also offer shoe repair making most dry-cleaning establishments a one-stop shop for all your outerwear care and needs.

Chapter 13

Shoes, Boots, and Footwear

FOR THIS CHAPTER, I tried to research how many footwear items we will go through in our lifetime. I didn't find any data for men, but I did find some interesting data for and about women. Some of the data I uncovered stated that during a woman's lifetime, she will spend about $20,000 on shoes. I figure that for boys and men, that figure is about half, or $10,000. I also found that on average, most women own twenty-seven pairs of shoes. While on average, a man will own twelve pairs of shoes.

I own thirty-four pairs of shoes and boots combined. That number has been reduced from the over forty pairs of shoes that I used to own because my wife made me throw out some of my shoes, or donate them to the local clothing drives.

As adults, we tend to overly compensate on material things that we didn't have as children. Thus is my case when it comes to shoes. As a child in sixth grade of elementary school, I dealt with such an issue. I learned to glue and stitch some of the soles of my shoes. One year, I had a pair of shoes where the sole of the shoe has separated from the top of the shoe, and when walking, the sole would flap and make an embarrassing noise. My solution to this problem was to wear a rubber rain overshoe over my school shoes. Every day, I'd pray that it would rain, so as not to be embarrassed by my classmates making fun of me. My classmates never teased me on the issue, thank God. Perhaps, twenty years later, I discovered that I was making a fashion statement without knowing it. I discovered that winter footwear and boots were available with a molded rubber base on shoes and boots to keep them waterproof.

As the young beginning consumer of footwear, I'd like to make a few suggestions to you that will, in the long run, save you tons of money while at the same time keep you looking as if you're in tune with the latest fashions. I realize that I'm facing an uphill battle because it is my words and deeds against your peers as to what is the most current trend and look. In stating that, I ask you, "Do you want to be a follower or a leader in setting the future fashion statement?" The follower will have no problem spending $85 or more to buy the latest sneakers just to fit in with his peers. In the past, it has always been those rebels who have defied the current trends, like James Dean and Marlon Brando that set the stage for their peers to follow them.

A coworker friend of mine told me that his grandfather told him, "You have to take care of your dogs." Translated, it meant that you have to take care of your feet. Buying shoes that are too small for your feet will never do you any good. They will hurt, and you'll not want to wear them for that fact.

When looking for a new pair of shoes, I would encourage you to look at the inside tongue of the shoe, or inside printing that gives you the size of the shoe and perhaps, more importantly, the materials that the shoe is made of. Although cheap shoes may offer the latest styles at the cheapest price, this is not always your best deal.

I always look to the tongue and side printed information prior to purchasing any new shoe. If the tongue, or inside labeling states, "All man-made materials," I immediately put them back on the shelf. Man-made materials may look good, but they are not good for your feet. Pleather, as it is sometimes called, is plastic that may look like leather. Plastic or pleather uppers will make your feet sweat and, in winter, will crake from the cold temperatures. In short, these shoes are lucky if you get a season or two out of them before they need to be replaced.

Perhaps your best bet is to only look for shoes that offer all-leather uppers or fully leather shoes or boots. Most of my readers are perhaps too young to remember the fashion trend of the platform shoe. This shoe offered a twice or more thickness of the sole of the shoe, and for the shorter men in our society, this shoe gave them a perceived look of being just as tall as the average man. The fad lasted for only a few years, and after the few-year period, anyone wearing them was a dated person linked to that period.

Just as with the rest of the exterior clothing that we wear, it is always the classics that stand out and become the true measure of what style is all about. The classics, as in clothing and shoes, will always hold up to the test of time. Additionally, most, if not all, of the classics have a better-than-built-in quality to them in terms of craftsmanship and the materials used to make them.

In the 1960s, America was hit with what was called the British invasion of new rock star groups, like the Beatles that took the American youth by storm. The music that they produced is still going strong to this day. Along with the music that they brought to America was their style of dress, and part of the apparel was an item of shoe that became known as Beatle boots. That style of half shoe / half boot is still popular today, although it might not be called by the same name. Thus, another classic came to be in the world of shoes.

As young adults, we all struggle with trying to identify and figure out what works best for us as individuals in style and perhaps presentation. Hopefully, I can help you to get through this process by pointing out to you what I think are the best practices and principles. Some of you feel at your best when wearing sneakers and/or your favorite pair of sneakers while there are others of you who don't feel completely dressed unless you have on your favorite pair of boots.

At some time in your life, the sneakers, or boots just aren't going to cut it for the dressed-up image that you need to present, and it is here that I say that the well-dressed man must have an over-the-top dress shoe. I've watched on television the Grammy's, Oscar's, and Emmy Awards more than once. One of the most appalling things that I've witnessed over the years is to see an announcer or recipient of an award come on stage in a tuxedo wearing a pair of sneakers. In addition to calling it a bad call by the wearer, I'd like to add that the two styles of dress just don't mix. I'd also like to say that if, for medical reasons, you have to wear sneakers as opposed to dress shoes that I do understand. Other than that which I have just stated, wearing sneaker to any formal event is just in very poor taste.

Getting back to guiding you as to the best values and choices on your building of a shoe collection that will serve you well for years to come. I'd like to first point out that if you only own one or two pairs of shoes that you wear on a regular basis, you'll quickly learn that shoe replacement comes to you more often than if you own more shoes or boots than you need. As time goes on, all shoes will wear out beyond all repair, and replacement becomes a necessity. By owning more shoes and rotating them, you'll find that you won't have to purchase for years.

I'd like to start with my own best places to purchase shoes. I don't have an issue with buying quality used shoes of great quality from places like eBay, or new shoes again of quality from online. In fact, most of my best shoe purchases have come from online. However, I do realize that some of you out there would never dare to wear used shoes. To that, I'd suggest that you search out the clearance sections of the major brands websites to get your best value. Along that line of suggestions I would advise that you stick with some of the tried-and-true classics in men's dress shoes. My suggestions are listed below.

The loafer—an Italian loafer is my first choice, the one with the tassels on the exterior of the tongue of the shoe. This shoe is often made of a woven leather on the toe and sides of the shoe. I'd buy three of this style of shoe: one in black, one in a brown tone, and one in a burgundy. This shoe offers you a very breathable stylish look that can be worn with everything from blue jeans, a sports jacket, and a three-piece suit.

The oxford has been a classic for decades and has derived a reputation as being man's staple as the formal dress shoe. For the beginner, I suggest that you only purchase a black wing tip oxford, followed at a later date with a brown, or burgundy wing tip oxford. An unbeatable men's dress shoe that will last you for decades and seem to never go out of style.

Sandals—at some point in every man's life, he is going to have a need town, or wear a pair or two of sandals. If one were to look and to stand apart from their peers, or even be the new trendsetter that you are, I'd suggest a woven pair of closed-toe sandals that could be worn at the beach or to the local clam bake on the beach and can even be worn to that afterhours bar or to the friend's afterhours house gathering and still be in style or above your peers in your own presentation of yourself. Very simple but yet very effective. You're not limited to just owning one pair of this vestal casual shoe. In fact, during the high heat of the summer, I've been known to wear a pair of my closed woven sandals to the office with a suit, and not only was I not criticized but praised by my peers in the office at work. Simply put some of our original can either work completely against us or work completely in our favor. We just need to be willing to take that chance to see what works for us, or against us as we travel through life.

Boots—in the Southwest and Midwest, cowboy boots serve a dual purpose of being the work boot of the day out on the range and perhaps herding cattle back into the safety of a corral for the night. Or for a night out on the town mixing with the locals at the latest bar, or bistro. Cowboy boots made their way back East during the Western look of the late sixties and early seventies among the city dwellers that were looking for their own way to stand out on the latest fashion pattern going on in the east.

Work boots also had their heyday among the city dwellers in the east with a brand called Timberland as the most popular work boot on the market. The bad backdrop in the media was that inner-city youth were being held up, sometimes at gunpoint, for their boots. This created a very negative image to the consumer who was not willing to place their life over the label of perhaps was a very fine product. In the end, that negative image might have been the downfall of the company's loss in revenues of a very good product.

Chapter 14

Manners, Posture, and Résumé

HAVING GOOD MANNERS and good posture will carry you a lot further in life than not possessing these qualities. Good manners begin at a very early stage in our lives, provided that we were blessed with the right parents, teachers, and mentors as we were growing up. The same holds true with our posture and how we carry ourselves. As for the unlucky few, you're going to have to educate yourself. Your local library is a great place to borrow books on the subjects at no cost to you. The second-best place to learn is the Internet. Again, at no cost to you. The benefits of self-educating yourself on these subjects is worth millions as far as an investment into your future is concerned.

Good manners goes far beyond just holding a door open for someone, regardless of their station in life while they are entering, or exiting your local convenience store. Good manners also go beyond just saying yes, sir, no, sir, or yes, ma'am, no, ma'am. To that later point, younger women have shown opposition to being called ma'am. I use the term young lady regardless of the woman's age. Elder women love being called young lady regardless of the circumstances because it conjures up a period in their lives when they were young, joyful, and hopeful of their futures.

Bad manners is jumping in front of a line of people at the grocery store. If the person jumping the line is young, then perhaps you could give them a pass because they just haven't been schooled in proper manners. But if the person jumping a line is in their sixties (as just happened to me), then you can conclude that this person is just rude.

My second wife had a saying with regard to a person speaking out, prior to thinking of what they were saying and how that might be interpreted by the listener. "It's far better to keep one's mouth closed than to open it and remove all doubt." What she meant by that saying were several things. First, we have two ears, and we can learn more by keeping our mouths shut and listening more. Secondly, if we haven't fact-checked the information that we are about to deliver to our listeners, we could find ourselves in a situation of trying to explain or defend what it is that we have just said, which, if not completely knowledgeable on the subject matter, could find ourselves in a very embarrassing situation that could threaten our credibility in the delivery of what we might want to convey in the future.

Bad manners—regardless of the past environment that we may have grown up in, we are all capable of making changes in our lives as we go forward in life. As I've said before, if we're guilty of an ill-doing, we don't stand a chance of correcting it until someone else brings it to our attention. At that very point, we have the power to make changes in our behavior or remain the same as we've always been. If we change our behavior, it means that we've learned from our past mistakes. But if we've ignored the new information passed onto us, then we have failed ourselves on the whole learning curve and will remain status quo.

The bad manners that I would encourage you to drop are curse words, racist words, or statements, and words like calling someone else sport because that very word conjures up an image of a person wearing a plaid sports jacket with perhaps binoculars and a horse racetrack program in their hand.

My own personal experience was when I was in an inside sales position of a company called Industrial Utilities Corp in the mid-1970s that was based in Brooklyn, New York, Long Island, New York, and New Jersey. I was taking sales orders over the telephone dealing with many of our existing customers in the industrial supply business, which supported many US manufacturers for their operating materials and equipment needs.

One day, I was taking an over-the-phone order from a purchasing agent named Chuck that I knew from many prior over-the-phone orders for the Reynolds metal plant in Rahway, New Jersey. At the end of his request for supplies, I thanked Chuck for his business by saying, "Thank you, sport." My boss overheard my closing statement, and he made me call Chuck back to apologize for calling him sport. Prior to calling him back, my boss conveyed to me the association of the term as I've described above. I called back Chuck and, instead of apologizing, asked him if he was offended by my closing statement and explained to him that my boss found it offensive. Being about twenty-three years of age, I didn't get the full ramification of my boss's point of view and, in hindsight, cooped out on my apology. Lesson learned, for sure. Thank God that the purchasing agent gave me a pass because it could have meant losing a major account of ours. On hindsight, my lesson was learned that what we say and that words do matter. It is with great hope that my own past experiences that I've shared with you throughout this book will be absorbed to the point that you don't make the same mistakes that I did on my learning curve.

Getting back to the bad-manners subject, also avoid using such terms as chump, boy, or any other current slang saying. This not only speaks to what we may say verbally but perhaps even more so speaks to our telephone manners, e-mail manners, and what we post on the social media sites, like Facebook, LinkedIn, Twitter, and on a number of other not-named sites with venues come back to bite us in the ass.

You can either let it go or confront the person and make them aware of their ill-doing. They will have a chance to correct their behavior or become confrontational. You'll have to decide is it worth it or not to educate this person or not. My advice is to let it go and not risk the drama. As Dale Carnegie wrote in his book *How to Win Friends and Influence People*, "A man convinced against his will is of the same opium still." One last bit of advice on manners would be to try and curb the use of profanity in terms of using it as an adverb, or an adjective when trying to describe a situation.

When I was a teenager back in the 1960s, the whole job-search scene was completely different from what it is today, and it, too, will change in the future as well as almost everything else. In high school, students could get a job in the community by getting working papers from the school guidance counselor, who would also provide you with an employment lead as well. After high school, most people got a job by word of mouth through a friend or by searching the want ads in the local newspaper. I didn't know what a résumé was until I came out of the United States Army in 1971. Another source for job searches was the Veterans Administration or the local community college. After college and a few jobs, I noticed that the human resources departments of most companies wouldn't dare to entertain an interview without receiving a prior résumé in the mail, or dropped off in person.

Today, the dynamics of seeking employment have changed once again. Nowadays, most companies will only accept your application for employment if it's remitted on their online portal. Another change that you may or may not be aware of is what I call résumé computer screening programs. Allow me to explain. Every job has a job description, and as part of that job description, there are keywords that pertain to that job or that industry. In some cases, certain industries have their own language with regard to the industry. If you don't know the language, you won't get the job. Perhaps this is why most people stay within the same industry when seeking another career change. Lots of companies now use abbreviations on the job to shorten the time needed to convey their message from one employee to another employee. This is a skill that most of you already possess due to your generation of texting.

In the federal government, in addition to the job description, which outlines the expected day-to-day duties of a position so that the applicant has knowledge of what is expected of them, the agency might also apply KSAs (knowledge, skills, and abilities) as part of the application process to see how much you know about the industry. A KSA question will be worded in such a way to see by your answer if you have experience into a given area.

The computer screening process will search for what I call buzzwords in your résumé and KSAs. The more buzzwords that match, the better qualified you will be for the position you are applying for, and the greater your chances are of being granted an interview. The HR field refers to this system as ATS (applicant tracking system), or ARS (automated résumé screening). Just as there are dozens of screening software programs out there to help the HR departments filter through résumés searching for the best-matched candidate for a position, there is likewise an equal number of websites out there that will teach you how to counter the automated systems so that your résumé is selected for an interview. Today, more than 60 percent of companies use automated résumé screening.

Let's jump forward to say the year 2050, which is only thirty-two years away. Most of your age group will still be in the job market. Now let's say that you have gotten past the Internet résumé screening process. Now let's say you're faced with the final stage or step in securing your new high-paying future job. If the past is any indication of what will be in the future, I can almost guarantee you that the personal interview process will change again. Just remember my old quote, "As time goes on, you'll pay more and get less."

If you're like most people, you can't visualize the future of five years, ten years, or fifty years away. Although most successful people do see future trends way before their peers, they are not just looking at what is happening now but are focused on looking at the past, current, and future information to kind of predict future trends and events.

You've passed the first two sets of tests that the corporation has placed in your way of getting a decent-paying job with future growth potential. Now you're faced with the final stage, which can catapult you from rags to riches. You know how the game has been played in the past and think to yourself that you are a shoo-in for this new position.

However, there is one factor that you may have failed to take into consideration. That factor is technology and how it affects even the smallest segments of our lives that we fail to take notice of and can have the greatest impact of our lives.

This day can have a whole major impact on the direction of your future. Now let's pretend that over time, you have learned how the whole hiring and place-ment system worked in the past. You're confident that you're due to get the job. However, the parameters of the past have changed, and you are no longer dealing with human beings as the interviewer but a half human / half cyborg that is reading everything about you from your clothes to your body language.

The human interviewer may pick up on the subtle aspects of your personality and what you have to offer to the company as far as growth or interactive ways of saving the company thousands of dollars. However, the cyborg half of the interviewer might be programmed to pick up on the slightest aspects of your attire. For example, the trained cyborg part of a human may be able to pick up on the fact that the tie bar or tie tack you're wearing is not of the highest quality and that your shirt is not of Egyptian cotton and that your suit is of a lesser quality. This simple technologic analysis of a half human / half cyborg can make or break a deal of thousands of dollars in salary. If your attire says cheap, then perhaps the salary they offer you might be less than what you're worth.

Forget the cyborg interview for now and consider a few changes in the hiring process that are happening right now and with changes to come within five to ten years. It's all about being prepared for the future, and knowledge is power. Drug testing was completely unheard of back in the seventies, and yet it is a common practice today among employers.

Imagine that your interviewer has a small camera mounted on their desk that is wired or wireless to a computer program. Now imagine that during your interview this camera is recording your every movement and is picking up on the fact that you're fidgety, restless, or anxious. Consider that the camera has an inferred lens on it, and it's also recording your heat signature, maybe even your pulse and heart rate. Suppose new technology now allows for lie detectors to read and record your answers to questions with no wires attached to you and without your knowledge. Now think of all this information going to a computer program and processing your language, eye movement, signature, and vital statistics to rate you with a score as a candidate for a position. It is very possible that they are already working on this new AI (artificial intelligence) today and that it might very well be commonplace in the future. How well would you fare in landing a job, or career with a company?

Even if you've done everything right, there is still no guarantee you are going to get the position, or get hired for another position. Dressing in the finest of clothing and creating that image of quality can sometimes backfire on you. I was once turned down for a job at a case tractor dealer because I was dressed too nice for the interview, even though I knew how to research parts and get pricing. On my second interview, my interviewer stated that he had no room for a prima donna. It could have been that he was concerned that I might replace his position.

Perhaps you're familiar with the Steve Jobs movie on the story of Apple computer. In the first half of the movie, it depicts Steve Jobs entering a conference room where he is to interview some potential employees. Steve Jobs entered the room wearing a T-shirt and blue jeans as I recall. The persons to be interviewed were dressed in white shirts and black ties. Mr. Jobs goes on to humiliate all the potential employees in the presence of others in the room. Steve rants on about the way the interviewees are dressed and tells them that they should be applying for jobs at IBM (International Business Machine), and in fact, they did have the dress code required by IBM. Steve Jobs was seeking out-of-box thinkers to work for his company and used his own dress code as the way his employees should dress for the job. I know that Steve Jobs was brilliant as an inventor and had lots of product visions that he brought to the marketplace; however, he failed miserably on his delivery to future employees. One of the business world's golden rules is we "phrase in public and criticize in private." The smarter tactic would have been to take each individual candidate into a private office one by one and explain to them why he didn't feel they would be a smart fit or suited for his company. Had Steve Jobs taken that approach, he may have found them to be very useful to his company later on down the road when he himself was fired from his own company. "Is it the clothes that make the man, or is it the man that makes the clothes"?

Chapter 15

Location, Location, Location

WHEREAS YOU MIGHT not think that this chapter may offer as much significance as any other prior chapters that I've written, but you might find yourself grossly mistaken. The apparel that you choose to wear at any given occasion can make, or break your forward future prospects of advancement. In some cases, what you choose to wear to any event can be the determining factor to your own future as to whether you advance or recede in your own circle of life.

Our youth have a tendency to dismiss that our actions of today will not impact us in the future. This is so far from the truth that it is almost laughable. Just ask any politician if their actions of their past haven't come back to haunt them today.

You'll find that most of them will have regrets of their past actions that they at the time perceived to be completely innocent.

American values do change over time. With that, what might have been an acceptable form of behavior in the past is not a necessary and acceptable behavior going forward into the future.

Please, think prior to acting upon your uneducated beliefs that what you do, or say today can very well impact, or even destroy what you do in the future.

The subject of this chapter is called "Location, Location, Location." In the retail environment, that very statement can mean the life, or death of any company. Pick the wrong location, and your company is starved for customer income, which means that your company will fail because of a lack of that income stream that is needed to keep your company afloat.

That customer income is required to meet and exceed your overhead capital requirements, advertising cost, and raw materials to produce the retail goods to bring to the retail marketplace.

My chapter of "Location, Location, Location" is to remind you to think of what location, or event that you might be attending. Although you might have a tendency to think that some events that you attend will have an impact on your current, or future standing in life, I can assure you that your thinking is totally wrong.

Let's say you've been invited to a football Super Bowl party by one of your friends. You want to attend, and perhaps, you know of some of the people that might be attending this party at one of your friend's homes. You could just go, or you could also decide to just throw on something that feels the most comfortable to you, or just with your current clothing that you're wearing.

Here is where I'm asking you to think outside the box of what at the time is considered normal by whatever current trend is going on in the fashion world. I'd like for you to just take a moment to think about the vast majority of your friends that might be attending this casual event. I'd like you to envision what your friends might be wearing to such an event. Furthermore, I want you to be able to stand out from the regular coward. Your style, if different from the rest of the herd, will make you a trendsetter as opposed to a follower.

In nature among the birds, it is the most flamboyant display of the birds that get the most females. I'm not asking you to take that route of being flamboyant. I also don't support or reject the styles of gay men or the whole LBGT community and their own right to the styles that they choose. It's just not my style.

But getting back to nature, you could attend that Super Bowl party, just like the average Joe. In the evening, you'll go home, just like the average Joe. However, if you think and if you dress beyond that of the average Joe, you'll be applying the laws of attraction by standing out from all your peers. People will have a tendency to want to gravitate toward you rather than repel against you.

In short, this means that you might be sleeping with your high school prom queen before the night is over or meeting the CEO of a major corporation that is offering you a six-figure job, all because you gave some thought to the way that everyone was going to present themselves and you decided to go just a little rogue and bump up your style, making yourself more approachable to conversation, which opened up doors that you thought were closed to you. People have a tendency to gravitate toward other people that they perceive to already be successful and tend to shy away from what might be a preconceived notion of who they are simply by the way that they are dressed.

In my chapter of "Location, Location, Location," I'd like to address to you the high school class reunion. Most, if not all, of us have been invited to the class reunion of our graduating class year from high school.

Times have changed, mindsets have changed, and so has the perceptions of what the most popular girl in school at the time was seeking that, perhaps at that time, we just didn't measure up to.

It's been long said that females are more advanced than men during the formative teenage years. I believe that statement to be completely true.

But by the same token, I must say that young girls are, as it seems to be, most attracted to the rebels, or nonconformist of any current society's rules.

I think this because these young women seek adventure and rebellion beyond what their fathers stood for.

To the young impressionable woman, it offers an element of excitement that her peers, or parents just can't deliver, and therefore, the excitement and allure exists.

However, over time, most young women realize that although these fun bad boys do fill a gap in their own rebellious behavior at a time that it is most needed by these rebellious young women, they seem to all come, or overcome to their senses that this type of male person is not the person that offers the stability of a home to rear their young. For this very reason, most of these women don't marry the bad boys that they were attracted to in the past but choose to marry the stable good boy that can provide the home, income, and stability of a growing family going forward into the future.

With the above said, if you have an invite to a high school class reunion, say, ten to twenty years later, you do not want to attend such an affair in the period of dress or style that was popular at that time. If you do dress in that time period, others will look at you as being dated and living in a time warp, which will do nothing for you in terms of making your old classmates want to gravitate toward you but most often shy away from you because they will clearly see that you've not advanced with the current times.

I don't give you all this above information so that you can meet and make out with your prom queen crush of years past but for you to present, or represent the whole new package that you've developed over the years of your own style and knowledge that you've obtained by being yourself and not being a follower to the current herd (in animal sense).

If you've decided to follow my advice throughout my book and decide to attend one of these events, you might be shocked to find that some of the most attractive people that blew you off in the past might be the most attractive to you and what to engage you in conversation. Even the jocks of the day, who might have lost their glory days, might be drawn toward you because you're delivering an aura of success, just by your outward appearance of the way that you've decided to dress for the occasion. You don't have to be successful in your field of work when going out to a public event, but looking the part of being successful can create the laws of attraction, which can open doors that were previously closed. The aura of perception perceived by others can and will make you more approachable to converse with you over others because you've shown by your outward appearance that you are already successful and don't need them. That very fact creates a gravitational pull of drawing them closer to you, making it easier for you to hone in on their needs and your own business needs of obtaining information that can be of value to you or not. At that point, you have the power to decide if you like this person as a friend or a business partner.

As I mentioned earlier in my book that most women will get dressed up just to go to the grocery store, they do that because they want to be prepared for any chance encounters that could happen, and they want to have their best foot forward. Social standing being what it is. I've personally observed that certain grocery stores tend to attract their women customers that are not seeking to raise their bar of dress and will go out wearing whatever they feel like with total disregard to the image they are sending out to the other patrons of the store. Without naming any of the grocery store chains, I'll just say that, for the most part, they tend to be major discount stores.

By the same token, the higher-priced grocery stores that offer a host of specialty items seem to attract a higher percentage of classier well-dressed women to their stores. Location does play a part with regard to the different types of people that you'll come into contact with. As young men, you might not have as many chances to visit your local grocery store, but regardless of whether it's a grocery store, department store, or auto parts store, you need to pay strict attention to the way that you dress and the image and signal that you're sending out to others.

What you're trying to do is to make yourself approachable by others that will want to engage in a conversation with you. By conversing with others, we stand to gain new knowledge, contacts, or leads that can enrich our lives in one way, or another. Look at the way you're dressed as a form of advertising. The saying is that advertising leads to sales, and sales lead to profit. By opening up the door of your willingness to converse with a complete stranger, you are now doing your own sales pitch. Simple chitchat at first can lead to a more in-depth advanced conversation that could benefit you greatly. You could discover that you have nothing in common with this new person that you've just met. But if you become a great listener and show good manners toward the other person, you leave them with a positive indelible mark of remembrance of you. It could also be that when they get home that they talk you up as being the nicest person that they met to their friends. It could also be that you run into this person in the future and that they share with you a whole host of positive information.

I also mentioned to you earlier in this book about having to go to the doctor's office, or hospital emergency room and that your exterior dress image could determine the type of care that you might receive. If your dress code says, "I'm poor and don't have the ability to pay," you might not receive the best service. Granted neither your doctor, nor the hospital can turn you away from service, but if you have to stay at the hospital, you might be placed into a room at the back of the building that has a view of a brick wall and rooftop of an adjoined building.

By the same token, if you're well-dressed, it says, "I have the ability to pay for all the services that you offer." An overnight stay for observation purposes might land you in a room in the front of the building with a view of the lake and fountain.

The same can hold true of checking into a hotel while on the road. Dressed well could mean that you get extra perks at no additional charge or an upgraded room at the economy rate. You might ask yourself why a hotel would do that. The answer is simple. Hotels, like any other business, would want to have a solid customer base of repeat customers. On top of that, they also know that word of mouth is the best advertising, so even if you don't get another chance to stay at another one of their hotels, the positive experience that you had when shared with your friends and coworkers can mean future business for the hotel chain.

Customers that look like they haven't taken a bath in weeks and deliver themselves as poor, or uneducated could find themselves paying a higher price for the hotel room and getting one of the worst rooms that they have because subconsciously, they don't want your business and so it most probably will be that you'll also receive the least amount of service. As people, we read other people all the time. Even if you're well-dressed doesn't ensure that you'll receive the best service at a hotel. If you happen to be one of those customers that are obnoxious, disruptive, or demanding, you could be one of the best-dressed people in town but that doesn't make up for the fact that you have bad manners. The hotel could decide that they don't want you as a customer regardless of how rich or well-dressed you are. Hotels, like any other business, also have an image in terms of who they are, just as we do.

Something else that I'd like to add to my area of conversing with others is to be engaging with complete strangers that you newly meet. That area is your body language when conversing with others;

whereas, your wardrobe applies the laws of attraction of making people be drawn toward you, or want them to repel away from you.

Your body language also speaks volumes in terms of whether you're interested in or engaged with anything that they may have to say or share with you. If the conversation is of any interest to you, you'll want to encourage the speaker to go forward. Keeping that in mind, I'd suggest to you that you treat any stranger that is looking to create a dialog with you that you give them your full attention.

This means making eye contact with them and showing the speaker your interest in what they have to say. At this point, it's more important that you listen more than you speak. Don't interrupt the speaker and wait for your own turn to speak and deliver your own message of the direction that you would wish the subject matter to go.

If your connection with this other person is perceived that you're wading away from what they have to say, they'll withdraw from speaking and end the conversation. But if you give them your undivided attention, you'll keep them engaged with a want to share even more information with you.

I'd like to take this time to talk a little about uniforms. Uniforms today are not just associated with blue-collar jobs. In fact, there is an equal amount of white-collar uniforms, although most of us don't easily pick up on the white-collar uniforms. For example. The front desk clerk at the hotel that you check into might be wearing a suit and tie that is his uniform. Some hotel chains and real estate supply their workers with a blazer-type jacket to have uniformity within their national chains.

What makes the difference of some uniform wearers excelling in their jobs, or careers? While other employees seem to remain stagnant and don't seem to advance at all within the company has more to do with how an individual wears or displays the uniforms that he is given. You might be saying, "How is that possible?" A uniform, like any other piece of clothing that you might wear, is almost like a neon sign. Customers and middle/upper management will all take notice to your presentation. It doesn't matter if you work for a car dealership, gas station, auto parts store, male nurse, movie theater, military, or fast-food business, What does matter is that presentation you give.

Wearing the company uniform, no matter what type, sends out a signal that either says, "I care about the way that I look, or I don't care about the way that I look" regardless of the type of uniform. If you show up to work in a dirty, wrinkled, torn uniform, you'll send the message of "I just don't care how I look." On the other side of the coin, if you show up for work in a clean, pressed, or better yet, starch pressed (perhaps even tailored) uniform, polished shoes, and clean-shaven appearance, then chances are you'll excel on the job. Everyone will notice, even your peers. You might even begin to notice that some of your coworkers try to emulate to you standard. I know that I've said this in the past, but I'm going to say it again. "Don't dress for the job that you have. Dress for the job that you want."

In bringing my first published book that I've ever written toward a close, I'd like to say that I could have written a six-hundred-page book on the subject matter that I've chosen to write about because the subject matter is so vast, and there is so much information available online to anyone.

I decided to limit my book to three hundred pages or less because I wanted it to be a convenient vessel that almost anyone could carry on their person, or in a tote. I also limited the size of my book because I didn't want to initiate by readers with too much information and have them get bored. If all goes correctly, as I look into the future I see the e-book and audiobook being distributed, which means you'll be able to view it or look up some area of interest on your smartphone.

It is with great hope that all my readers will be able to glean something from my book going forward that can be applied to their daily lives that enriches their lives for the better by attracting positive contacts that are drawn toward the outside image that they are projecting through their outer image by the use of the clothing that they choose to open doors for them that might have been blocked in the past by the mere image that their clothing and look was projecting. If my book information can change the lives of a hundred young men, then I've done my job of attracting conversation and approachability, which opens the doors of advancement as opposed to repelling it, then everybody wins.

It is with even greater hope that most of my readers will gain so much more and put into practice all that they have learned. There is nothing more I'd love than to see thousands of young men apply the principles of my book to their best advantage for their own success as they go forward into their own futures. That wishful thinking on my part creates a win-win-win situation for all. I'll archive success by knowing that I did something for enrichment of all our youth, the young readers and appliers will have enriched their own lives by gaining and applying newly learned knowledge, and society as a whole will also have gained by having productive, tax-paying, and law-abiding citizens as the mainstream of the American backbone of what we were once in the past and will become in the future again.

Going forward, our lives are based upon the choices and decisions that we make along that path. Sometimes we make the right choses and decisions, and we celebrate them. Other times, we make so-so decisions, which we might wait out to see if we made the right choice, or the wrong one. Lastly, we make bad decisions, and hopefully, we learn from these mistakes that we've made. If we haven't learned from our mistakes, we are due to repeat them until we have learned from them, or they will hold us back for the rest of our lives.

I'm sixth-eight years young. I state this because when I was in my twenties, as most of my readers are today, I said to myself in 1970, "In the year 2000, I'll be fifty years old." And just to share with you the foolish thinking of a younger person, I also used to say, "I don't want to ever get old." It took me a few years to understand what a foolish statement I was stating when I was younger and less self-educated than what I'm today. One day, I realized the stupidity of my firm belief at the time. Hey, Carl, wake up and smell the roses. If you don't get old, you get dead. That epiphany caused me to rethink my whole concept on getting older. From that point forward, I formed a totally new way of thinking about the whole aging concept and adopted a totally new way at looking at the same subject.

I formed this outlook of which I live by to this very day. No one knows when our time is up and when we will die. I formed a very simple mindset to help me live to a ripe old age. I first said, "I was born in 1950. Medicine is advancing faster than I'm aging." Second, I said, "No one knows what the cap is on aging." Third, I said, "I set a goal for myself to live to be 130 years of age, my reasoning being that if I don't set a goal of 130 years, I'll never make it to 110 years of age."

To some of you readers, the above might seem completely foolish, while others might see the wisdom in what I've stated. My point being that regardless of the end product that you're looking to achieve in your life, you have to set goals to reach where you want to get in your life. They can be personal, business, or anything in between. Sometimes you'll meet the goals you've set for yourself, other times, you might only make it halfway to the goal that you've set, and other times, you'll completely fail to even get close to the goal that you've set for yourself. But in the long run, if you haven't the mindset to set goals for yourself, you're doomed to fail.

It used to be that doctors treating cancer patients would tell their patients that were about to receive chemotherapy that they could expect the following side effects of weakness and having hair loss as a result of the treatment. Sure enough, all their patients got exactly what was described by what their doctors said.

Over time, some doctors changed the way that they delivered their message to their patients by creating a message to the mind of a more positive message and, as a result, started to see a remission and, in some cases, a complete recovery. I state all this to make the point of the fact of positive thinking and the seeds that are planted into our brains. To some of you readers, you might dismiss my reasoning as complete nonsense. But to others, they might see some validity to what I'm addressing.

Our minds and what we think and process along with the seeds that are planted into them cannot only have a mental effect on us but also a physical effect as well. The wrong input or stress upon our brains can develop one aspect. While a more-positive approach can produce an entirely different well-being result. I've adopted an approach and mindset for my own well-being. First off, let me tell you that the only drugs that I take is an antihistamine and only when I feel that it is needed. The same holds true with ibuprofen and aspirin. Outside the occasional antibiotic, I don't take any other medication. My mindset is that when I should feel ill, I will only take what I think will make me feel better. When I take the medication, I say to my mind that with the medication or without it that I'm summoning up a team of Pac-Men to obtain from the medication or from my own body what it is that they need to attack and defeat the invader to my body that is making me feel unwell. As a result, I feel better within days because I've planted the seed of a quick recovery to my mind and let my mind and body do all the rest. Just in case you didn't know, stress can produce physical signs and ailments in people where there is nothing physically wrong with them.

Perhaps you didn't need for me to go all into the whole mental and physical aspects that make up all of us. How we respond to that aspect will differ from all of us and our own mindset.

I want to leave all you with the most positive and helpful notes to promote you to the next level in your own evolution of success and achievement to better your life. In doing so, I have bulleted what I deem as the most-useful quotes and sayings.

Chapter 16

Pay Your Own Way in Life

I WOULD LIKE to believe that if you are between the ages of thirteen and thirty that more than likely, you've attended a rock concert. I just hope that I'm right on my assumption. Because if you've been to a concert, then you are more than likely familiar with the encore after a performance. The paying audience claps, or chants out to the performers that the audience is wanting more. That very pressure will cause, in most cases, the band to come back out onstage and give the paying audience one last encore, or set.

It is my belief that my readers are wanting something more at the end of my informative, educational book. I offer to you, my readers, what I consider perhaps the most valuable of all the information that I have delivered so far.

Without doubt, I consider this chapter to be of utmost importance to my readers and a bonus chapter that I only conceived of after I applied a copyright of my book as an unpublished manuscript to the end of my book. All things happen for a reason. This was the case of my deciding to add chapter sixteen. I added this chapter because I thought it so important.

Wake up, all you who are still under the age of thirty. Paying your own way in life means that you are not reliant upon others to house, feed, or support you in any way. For some of you, this concept has never been considered, and you have reached a comfort level of acceptance that somehow, others are required to pay your way in life. This is perhaps you've convinced yourself that you are somehow entitled to the benefit of others supporting you.

Allow me to deliver to you the cold hard truth. If you've been lucky enough to have reached the age of twenty-one by law, no one is responsible for your food, shelter (rent), debit, clothing, transportation, medical bills, and/or college (student loans).

If you're between the ages of twenty-one and fifty years of age and still living under your parents', or grandparents' roof, and you are not paying your own way as far as rent, utilities, and food. Then I consider you to be nothing more than a leech, moocher, or parasite to your host family. More than likely, your family has paid their dues in life and don't need to be burdened with a nonproductive member of society and their expenses.

I will excuse those individuals that have a bona fide physical, or mental disability, but for the rest of you, there is no excuse. Unless you are paying your supporting family back what you owe plus interest on what they could have made if they didn't take their savings to support you, I'll give you some grace. Sometimes life throws us a curveball, and we need to call on family as a last resort. Just make sure you do them right that have helped you out of your bind and not stick them with the bill of yours.

"It doesn't cost a million to look a million."

"We only get one chance to make that first impression."

"Quality never goes out of style."

"As time goes on, we will always pay more and get less."

"Some people know the price of everything but the value of nothing."

"Don't dress for the job that you have. Dress for the job you want."

"It's the ability to recognize and seize an opportunity that distinguishes the entrepreneur from the ordinary businessman."

"Body language speaks louder than we all might think."

"Image, honesty, and reputation is like virginity. Once we lose it, we may never get it back."

"A place for everything, and everything in its place [key to organization]."

"The turtle doesn't get anywhere until he sticks his neck out."

"Does life imitate art? Or does art imitate life?"

"A stitch in time saves nine."

"Nothing ventured, nothing gained."

"Beauty is in the eyes of the beholder."

"Are you a trendsetter, or a trend follower?"

"Fads and trends are short-lived, but true style goes on for decades."

"If you buy cheap, you'll get cheap, and it will not stand the test of time."

"We get what we pay for."

"Too smart too soon. Too wise too late" (youth versus old age and knowledge obtained).

"We don't know where we're going until we fully understand where we came from."

"First, that which precedes all others in time, order, and importance."

"Don't dress for the job that you have. Dress for the job that you want."

"Second sucks."

"Whatever you do, always aspire towards greatness."

"Time is money." (Use it wisely.) You have the power to determine who gets your money based upon what the business is providing and the customer service you receive. You are in the position of holding and controlling the power of your money. Don't feel bad if you walk away from a business that is not looking out for your needs but hold their own needs above your own. You can spend your hard-earned cash anywhere, and you have that power to decide who is going to get your hard-earned cash and who is not.

"Always pay yourself first." Meaning allow your paycheck to make money for you by investing to make you money while you're sleeping. In other words, get your money working for you as opposed to you working for your money (stocks, real estate, bonds, metals).

"The difficult, we do right away. The impossible takes a little longer."

"I have calluses on my hands, not on my ass" (by sitting around waiting for something to happen). I've yet to any man stumble upon anything while sitting around doing nothing. A body in motion tends to stay in motion while a body at rest tends to stay at rest. Give a person a task that seems to have all the time on their hands, and the task will not be completed. Give the same person a task that is busy, and it'll get done.

"A penny saved is a penny earned."

"I've yet to see anyone stumble upon anything while just sitting upon their ass."

"A body in motion tends to stay in motion while a body at rest tends to stay at rest."

"The early bird does catch the worm."

"Slow and steady does win the race" (regardless of how small your investments in savings). Over time, your small amounts will tend to lead toward larger amounts over time, which will place you into a position to have the available cash resources on hand to capitalize upon further investment opportunities that your peers just don't have the free assets available to move on.

"When everyone else is buying stock, you sell. When everyone is else is selling stock, you buy" (Warren Buffet).

"No, thanks. I'm trying to quit." A helpful phrase to let people know without doubt that you're not interested in their offer, or advice.

"You touch me like you know me." A way of delivering your message that someone is invading your own personal space.

The way that we deliver certain messages to others is a gift that we'll learn over time. Although not completely insulting, they will get the message. If delivered just right, it will leave them pondering your response with a "Did they compliment me? Or did they just insult me?"

"Nothing ventured, nothing gained."

"We get in life what we earn, or what we deserve" is based upon our own actions toward others.

"Honesty is doing the right thing when no one is looking." Meaning that we can sometimes do the wrong things in our lives if we don't think that we have a chance at never being caught by doing something that is dishonest. In most cases, we are seriously mistaken about our own judgment, which can come back to haunt us in the near, or distant future. Why risk such embarrassment?

"Live your life as if the day before were to be published on the front page of your local newspaper." And you would not be embarrassed by anything that was printed about you.

"To avoid regrets during your life-time," listen to what your gut is telling you what the right choice is. If it feels right, do it. If not, listen to your inner voice.

"When we get greedy, we generally wind up getting nothing."

"As poverty comes into the front door, love goes out the window." Meaning that most women marry for the security of themselves and their offspring, and when their man can't provide the basics of that, they are more than willing to look else-where to someone else who can provide the bare essentials of their needs for them and the children that they have borne.

"For everything that we get in our life, we give up something else in return." If you want more money, then be prepared to give up more of your free time to achieve it. If you're looking for more free time in your life, then be prepared to give up more of your income if working for someone.

The same holds true with being a treasure hunter, globe tracker, salesman, or anything else that is going to pull you away from your family. You'll be giving up your whole family foundation, or structure for the sake of chasing your own dreams.

"Advertising leads to sales, and sales leads to profit." Advertising through TV, print, web, or radio will let everyone in the viewing, or listening audience, or network know that you are out there making your voice, or media image to be heard and to attract the buyer of your goods, or services.

"The higher that we climb, the harder the fall." All that raises must fall in accordance with the laws and rules of gravity. Hence, it doesn't just apply to the climbing of a mountain as Mount Everest but also applies to the corporate world of business, Wall Street, or real estate. In short, the bottoms of all markets do come to bottom out, just as all markets tend to reach their peaks. "Hence, buy low, sell high" may make the most sense, but no one is able to predict the future of any market, regardless of how good they claim to be. It doesn't matter if it's metals, crops, crude, stocks, bonds, or real estate.

Although many have tried, it seems that the unexpected in most markets will rear its ugly head to defy any market. Even the most analytical experts have been left in awe with the complete reversal of market trends of the past that they perceived would not change but did.

Although most of my closing catch-phrases apply to many of the chapters that I've written throughout my book, I have added many coined phrases that I absorbed throughout my own life that I deem to be helpful for you going forward in your own life.

My book has been written to help you know of and avoid the pitfalls that I've had to learn in some cases the hard way. In my closing, it is my best hope that I've given all you the best advice of advancing your work and personal life and that the roads begin to open up to you for a greater standard of living than that which I have achieved.

I feel truly blessed from the many people that I've encountered and met along my own journey and the knowledge that they all so unselfishly shared with me for my own advancement in my life. To be able to go from an almost-dirt-poor environment to end up as upper-middle class and perhaps beyond that as I go forward into my own future is beyond my own wildest dreams. Paying it forward as I think that I'm trying to deliver with the writing of my first book. It is with great hope that all my readers excel beyond their wildest dreams to achieve all that they want and desire within their own lives.

My best to all you on your bargain hunting of your attire and presentation to others. With the continued hope that you'll be applying the laws of attraction to make other people want to engage with you in conversation, which can open up windows of learning, knowledge, and opportunities of contacts at present and going forward into the future. Keep those business cards that you collect along the way. Although they might not serve you in the present, they may help you going forward into your future.

About the Author

THE AUTHOR'S PRETEEN period, he was introduced to Paula Hutchison, a noted illustrator and writer of children's books. Paula took this budding young artist writer under her wing. She took great pride in teaching that unknown author all her wisdom and knowledge of the literary world that she had acquired over her lifetime and freely passed it onto a younger generation. It would be many years before this author would discover what a precious gift he had been given, only to be used in his own later years. The early training served him well as being a visual observer of everything around his. Taking in not only positive space but negative space as well to form a complete picture as to what was going on.

The author went on to obtain a liberal arts degree. He majored in art and minored in business. The literary world took a back seat as he found himself working in the business world of the private sector for over twenty years, then switching career paths to working for the federal government until his retirement in 2015.

9 781662 440823